A Psychodynamic View of Action and Responsibility

This new book by David Shapiro, author of the classic *Neurotic Styles*, throws light, from a clinical standpoint, on a subject of importance, both theoretically and for therapeutic practice, for psychoanalysts and psychotherapists, as well as for those with general interests in philosophy or psychology. *A Psychodynamic View of Action and Responsibility* explores the individual's experience of ownership or responsibility for what he or she does, says, and even believes, and their avoidance of that experience.

David Shapiro considers the self-deception necessary for these disclaimers of responsibility and the surrender of personal conviction and autonomous judgment. With numerous excerpts from therapeutic sessions, he shows these to be self-protective reactions forestalling or dispelling the anxiety of internal conflict and also, as in false confessions, external threat or intimidation. Shapiro presents this important thesis in his usual lucid way and in many contexts. Its recognition, in his view, is critical for therapeutic work. This book demonstrates the central place in psychological dynamics of the subjective sense of personal responsibility or ownership of what one says or does. The subject is nowhere treated with the depth and emphasis on subjective experience seen in these chapters.

A Psychodynamic View of Action and Responsibility will appeal to professionals and students of psychoanalysis and psychodynamic psychotherapy, as well as clinical psychologists, CBT practitioners, philosophers, and legal scholars.

David Shapiro is Professor Emeritus at the Graduate Faculty, New School for Social Research in New York City and practices psychotherapy in New York. He previously practiced psychotherapy in Los Angeles and taught at the School of Social Welfare, UCLA. He is the author of *Neurotic Styles*, *Autonomy and Rigid Character*, *Psychotherapy of Neurotic Character*, and *Dynamics of Character*.

A Psychodynamic View of Action and Responsibility

Clinical Studies in Subjective Experience

David Shapiro

LONDON AND NEW YORK

First published 2017
by Routledge
2 Park Square, Milton Park, Abingdon, Oxon OX14 4RN

and by Routledge
711 Third Avenue, New York, NY 10017

Routledge is an imprint of the Taylor & Francis Group, an informa business

© 2017 David Shapiro

The right of David Shapiro to be identified as author of this work has been asserted by him in accordance with sections 77 and 78 of the Copyright, Designs and Patents Act 1988.

All rights reserved. No part of this book may be reprinted or reproduced or utilised in any form or by any electronic, mechanical, or other means, now known or hereafter invented, including photocopying and recording, or in any information storage or retrieval system, without permission in writing from the publishers.

Trademark notice: Product or corporate names may be trademarks or registered trademarks, and are used only for identification and explanation without intent to infringe.

British Library Cataloguing in Publication Data
A catalogue record for this book is available from the British Library

Library of Congress Cataloging in Publication Data
Names: Shapiro, David, 1926– author.
Title: A psychodynamic view of action and responsibility: clinical studies in subjective experience / David Shapiro.
Description: Abingdon, Oxon ; New York, NY : Routledge, 2017. | Includes bibliographical references and index.
Identifiers: LCCN 2016057278| ISBN 9780415787703 (hardback : alk. paper) | ISBN 9780415787710 (pbk. : alk. paper) | ISBN 9781315225760 (e-book)
Subjects: LCSH: Autonomy (Psychology) | Responsibility. | Psychotherapy.
Classification: LCC BF575.A88 S53 2017 | DDC 155.2/5—dc23
LC record available at https://lccn.loc.gov/2016057278

ISBN: 978-0-415-78770-3 (hbk)
ISBN: 978-0-415-78771-0 (pbk)
ISBN: 978-1-315-22576-0 (ebk)

Typeset in Times New Roman and Gill Sans
by Florence Production Ltd, Stoodleigh, Devon, UK

To Eloisa

Contents

	Acknowledgments	*viii*
	Introduction	1
1	Two kinds of responsibility	15
2	The psychology of self-deception	27
3	Two kinds of conscientiousness	41
4	The self-control muddle	51
5	Will, willpower, free will	65
6	Neurotic styles	77
7	Schizophrenia	89
8	Saying something is doing something	105
9	Voluntary surrender of responsibility	119
	Afterword: Action and responsibility	129
	Index	*131*

Acknowledgments

I want to express my gratitude to Dr. Craig Piers of Williams College and Lenox, Massachusetts who read the manuscript carefully and critically more than once and made any number of helpful suggestions. I am grateful to Professor Louis Sass of Rutgers University who also read most of the manuscript and whose thoughtful comments have influenced me as they have in the past. I have had many valuable discussions of the subjects and the writing of this book with my son, Benjamin Shapiro, and I want to express my appreciation to him for that, as well as for his technical help in its preparation. My daughter, Julie Shapiro, was very helpful in the completion of this project, and I want to thank her for that. My friend, Jenny Penberthy, of Vancouver BC, also gave valuable help when needed. Finally, I want to thank my wife, Gerry Shapiro, for her encouragement and forbearance during this long project.

I want to acknowledge, with thanks, permission to reprint here the substance of two previously published articles. "Self-Reproach and Personal Responsibility" was originally published in the journal *Psychiatry*. "On the Psychology of Self-Deception" was originally published in the journal *Social Research*. Minor alterations have been made here to both.

Introduction

We live and experience ourselves in action. That is to say, autonomous, self-directed action. By a stretch we might say that all living things exist in action. This might be said even of the movement of a sunflower turning to follow the sun, but its action is sun-directed, not self-directed. It is in the conscious choices that we make, in what we choose to do or say, that we experience ourselves most keenly as autonomous beings. It is in those choices that we experience our action as ours, something that we initiated, for which we are responsible. So it is no wonder, when our action or our anticipation of it evokes personal anxiety or discomfort, that we want to disown it, try to avoid or disclaim our responsibility for it. It is no wonder that we try, sometimes consciously, sometimes unconsciously, in the course of that effort, to escape from the fact, or at least the experience, of our autonomy, even to surrender our critical judgment, to find direction elsewhere, or deny capability, and thus dilute our responsibility for what we do or say. That is what this book is about.

One can speak of autonomy or self-directed action in earliest infancy only in a limited sense. New infants, it is true, are innately considerably more purposeful than had once been thought. They are cognitively ready for interest in and response to their immediate surroundings. Infants are capable of nuanced sensory discriminations, recognition of repeated patterns and purposeful, coordinated action to bring about desired events. All this and more, but they are still short of consciously intentional action, action with a goal clearly in mind. That kind of action develops, instinctive reactions gradually become educated, with increasing cognitive, motor, and sensory capabilities. Thus, infants suck from the beginning, purposefully, but more or less reflexively; then, with pleasurable experience and increased competency, sucking becomes more intentional. They grasp the rattle at first when it is visibly close at hand, but an interest in it is developed and, with increased capabilities, they look and reach for the rattle. As the child's recognition of an external world becomes more extensive and more objective, new, more active relationships with things in the world are developed. The young child learns that the shiny round objects that he has seen can be played with. A new object of interest, marbles, has been created and at the same stroke a new, more active subject, a marble player, comes into being. Intentionality and deliberateness have developed further, and along with these some sense of personal capability and effectiveness. Each extension of the child's interests opens new possibilities of activity and each results in a more actively and consciously directed person. As the child's action becomes more deliberate he or she is more conscious of action itself. This development of increasingly deliberate and consciously articulate aims and purposes continues at least through adolescence. Deliberateness of purpose extends, for instance, to the adolescent's consciousness of their own authority over themselves, and to their often exaggerated assertion of that authority and independence of decision. They know what they want to do and are conscious that it is they who choose to do it. In exactly that sense, they are conscious of personal responsibility for their action.

Of course, not every action, even for the most serious and careful adult, is deliberate. Habitual, more or less automatic reactions are learned with practice and life experience. More important, the spontaneous ways that were predominant in childhood, carrying a fainter sense of responsibility, are not left entirely behind. Every individual has a variety of ways of action at his disposal: spontaneously reactive, habitual and virtually automatic, consciously intentional and deliberate in various degrees. And every person has a characteristic, not exclusive, but predominant, style of action: spur-of-the-moment for one, cautious and reflective for another. These ways of action are accompanied by particular qualities of subjective experience, different degrees of self-consciousness, differences in deliberateness or consciousness of intention, different levels of conviction in what one does or says. Many of these kinds of subjective experience can be discerned in the speech and manner of a speaker by an attentive observer. An absence of complete conviction, for instance, often shows itself in too loud an assertion of confidence or an uneasy or evasive look.

Given the place of action in life, one might easily imagine this matter, the various kinds of actions and their various kinds of subjective experience, to be a well worn one in psychology, but it is not. Academic psychology has limited itself by its concern with objectivity and in doing so it has neglected the study of subjective experience in general. More interest might have been expected from psychoanalysis, which is my own background, but that has not been forthcoming either. Then, too, the psychology of volitional action has been burdened by logical or philosophical problems surrounding the subject of free will and determinism. Where one might have expected psychological study to bring some light to that problem, just the reverse has happened; the philosophical problem has stalled psychological understanding. The wish to avoid vitalistic conceptions of a faculty of will capable of transcending psychological causes, and the problem of reconciling volitional experience with the scientific assumption of a lawful, predictable world of cause and effect, have had the effect of inhibiting approaches to the psychology of action, especially the variety and dynamics of its subjective experience. Psychoanalysis dispensed with vitalistic and moralistic conceptions of will and free choice and replaced them with an analysis of antecedent causes. Action, behavior, was understandable in terms of forces and agencies operating according to natural law. In principle, it was unarguable. It was no less than a principle of science. But the embodiment of this principle in psychoanalysis and other motivational psychologies led to the assumption that the individual is caused to act by internal forces and agencies according to directions or tendencies intrinsic to these forces and agencies (Shapiro 1970; Schafer 1976). We shall turn to this problem in Chapter 5 and again in Chapter 9. For the present, it is enough to note that in this conception conscious choice can have at most the status of an ill-explained subjective experience since it does not provide, but only reflects, the impetus and aims of action. The place of cognition in action is seen only as instrumental in guiding needs to their satisfaction.

Constrained in these ways, psychologists and psychoanalysts often describe action too simply as the product of needs, impulses or drives, or, in the cautiously progressive spirit of more recent psychoanalytic thought, wishes. But needs, impulses, drives, even wishes cannot account for action; they can account only for temptations. No sensible person will accept the argument of a defense attorney who says that the rape his adolescent client committed was on account of the strong libidinal desires to be expected at that age. Action is more complicated than that. Needs, impulses, or wishes do not have responsibility for action; people do. There remains, therefore, an incompleteness in this picture of motivation and action. What is missing or insufficient is the active, thinking person, not simply moved by inner forces or constrained by inner agencies, but making purposeful choices, sometimes deliberately, sometimes impetuously or even quasi-reflexively, in any case according to how they see things.

Let me give an example from psychiatry of the difference between the two views of the experience of action. It is in connection with a particular problem in the understanding of action, the problem of indecision: A well-known characteristic of the people we call obsessive is a psychological state in which they feel unable to choose between alternative actions, as between two movies or two items on the menu, or whether to pursue a particular course or abandon it. Often at such a moment the obsessive person will say that he cannot choose because the alternatives seem equally desirable or equally undesirable, or because a particular action is both attractive and repellent. From the standpoint of needs or wishes the problem appears, therefore, to be a quantitative one, a contest of forces. Consistent with this view, the problem of indecision has often been understood as a product of ambivalence, a contest of contrary needs or inner forces, presumably of equal strength, rendering the individual as though paralyzed, unable to move one way or the other. But this obsessive kind of indecision cannot be accounted for so simply. To begin with, an exactly equal balance of desirability and undesirability of any objective is unlikely on its face.

Obsessive indecision consists, rather, of an agonized alternating between one leaning and another, a process that is full of active, complicated, often quasi-moral thinking. It is a kind of thinking found in individuals characterized, whether they know it or not, by attitudes of a special kind, in particular a special kind of conscientiousness, which we shall consider in more detail in Chapter 3. According to this kind of conscientiousness, the obsessive person requires of himself a certain sort of ritual in making a decision. As if to be sure he does not do the wrong thing, he must confront himself repeatedly with all the arguments he can think of that are adverse to whatever action he momentarily favors. A leaning toward one side therefore prompts him to an active search for arguments favoring the other side. The individual becomes, for the moment, a proponent of what looks like the losing side. Typically, this search is continued until the leaning shifts, at which point the process is repeated in the other direction.

This is a person for whom the sense of responsibility for a personal choice of action, even when its objective consequences are trivial, is no light matter. On the contrary, it is the prospect of such a choice, of that autonomous act of personal freedom, that is sufficiently anxious or threatening as to cause him to shrink from it. We see this confirmed by his relief when the responsibility of a personal choice is removed by some conclusive external circumstance or, more commonly, if he can find some authoritative rule or judgment that seems to him decisive, something that determines in his mind what he should do. Relieved of the necessity of a personal choice, he might even be satisfied with either outcome. But he is not likely, then, to feel that he is choosing what he really wants or, to feel fully, personally responsible for the result.

In the late 1950s, as a young psychologist on the staff of the Austen Riggs Center, a distinguished psychoanalytic sanitarium, I encountered the work of the innovative psychoanalyst, Hellmuth Kaiser. Kaiser had been invited to speak to the small staff. I was impressed by his presentation and, also, by him and his quiet confidence. His topic was unusual. His presentation had to do with the way his patients in psychotherapy talked. Kaiser, not coincidentally, had been a student of Wilhelm Reich, who in his early, still psychological, teaching and writing had emphasized the importance of the therapist's attention not only to what the patient said, but to how he said it. Kaiser presented a clinical observation that I had never heard before, one that was subtle, yet at the same time striking. He had observed, he said, that his neurotic patients did not seem to be fully "behind" what they were saying (Kaiser, 1955). They did not seem to really mean it. Their speech did not seem to be genuinely expressive of what they actually thought or felt. It was regularly marked by a certain artificiality. Yet there was no suggestion of insincerity.

For example, a patient might say that he "thinks" he really wants to marry his girlfriend. He seemed to be trying to look happy, trying even to be happy, but he sounded more resigned than happy. Other patients were theatrical, also expressing emotions that seem forced and artificial. Still others described their problems in ways that sounded rehearsed. But, again, for the most part these people seemed quite sincere. They were not trying to deceive the listener; they were, though Kaiser did not put it this way, deceiving themselves. They were unknowingly playing a role, being or trying in some degree to feel or think or be something other than what they actually felt or thought or were. The result was a lack of conviction or wholeheartedness in what they said. As they spoke, they did not seem to completely vouch for what they, themselves, said. Kaiser described this phenomenon as the absence in the speaker of a sense of responsibility for what he was saying.

I had never heard, or heard of, this observation before, but once I considered it and observed my own patients with it in mind I was convinced of its accuracy. I think that any therapist or, for that matter, anyone, therapist or not, who listens to and watches a speaker closely can confirm the phenomenon, not in everyone certainly, and not even in neurotic patients with absolute consistency, but often enough to be convinced of its validity. If it has not been noted clearly before, it is likely because we are not accustomed to listening to people in that way. We, psychotherapists included, are used to paying attention to the content of a speaker's words, much less so to his attitude toward his words.

Kaiser regarded this phenomenon as a reflection of the rift in the neurotic person's personality, his estrangement in various degrees from what he feels or thinks. There is no doubt that it is that, that such estrangement exists in neurotic conditions and that it is reflected in this way. But, as we will see, a diminished sense of responsibility for what one says and does is more than a reflection of a more fundamental process. For it is also the individual's retreat from, avoidance of, the experience of his own presence. It is not hard to understand such a retreat as a self-protective response to the anxiety of personal expression, decision, and action. This phenomenon is most evident in neurotic people, but it surely holds in some measure for all people. In other words, under certain conditions, internal as well as external, a retreat from full expression of oneself to a different state of mind, a retreat from genuine conviction in and responsibility for what one does or says, or even believes, may be protective against the anxiety of personal choice, decision, and judgment. Under externally threatening conditions it may be unsafe not only to say what one believes, but even to allow oneself to believe it, and it may seem so under certain internal conditions as well.

Apart from external constraints humans are, objectively, autonomous, volitional, creatures. One imagines that autonomous action, choosing what one wants to do, must include a satisfying experience of personal freedom, and a further satisfaction that what one has done has been of one's own choice. Yet people do not always feel that freedom of choice, nor that what they have done is what they chose to do. Sometimes people persuade themselves that they are doing what they really want to do when actually they are doing only what they think they should or what is expected of them; and sometimes, when people do what they really want to do, they find it necessary to disavow their responsibility for doing it, even to themselves. In many different ways and to different degrees people often do not feel, and do not want to feel, that their actions are completely theirs, wanted and chosen and intended by them. They sometimes think that they have acted unwillingly, though their action was not forced by circumstances. Assigning responsibility elsewhere, they may think that they were driven or compelled by some internal requirement that they repudiate, but cannot resist. The drinker says ruefully, "I don't know how to refuse," the impetuous individual says, "I'm ruled by my emotions," the officer, explaining assaulting a provocative prisoner, says, "The adrenaline takes over." In ways like these, sincere people disavow full responsibility for their action. In those ways, they do not experience themselves as autonomous beings saying what they mean and doing what in some sense they want and intend to do. Sometimes reactions like these are situational, limited to specific circumstances or specific actions; sometimes they are quite general expressions of the dynamics of the personality. Sometimes their effects are entirely individual, manifest only in personal traits or the quality of personal relationships. But sometimes the retreat from, or surrender of, genuine conviction and responsibility for action is evident not just in individuals, but in groups and with accordingly wider consequences.

The book does not cover its general subject systematically, but there is a certain logical succession to its chapters. It is especially desirable to read the first chapter, "Two kinds of responsibility," first. The distinction that I make there will help to avoid a misconception about the meaning of responsibility as it is used primarily here. The distinction is between the meaning of responsibility as moral accountability, which in the case of failure is often accompanied by self-reproach and shame, and its meaning simply referring to one's action as having an effect. For convenience here, I call the latter the psychological meaning, as opposed to the moral meaning, of responsibility; its subjective quality may also be described as a sense of agency or authorship of action. The philosophical literature on responsibility, as far as I am aware, has mainly to do with moral responsibility or accountability. Responsibility for action in the sense of its cause has been regarded as simply a matter of fact. Objectively, that is certainly justified. Our interest here, however, is in the subjective experience of this objective fact, and that is far from simple. The use in this chapter of an exchange in the psychotherapy of a person in a crisis in which both kinds of responsibility play a part will sharpen that distinction. Actually, the example does more. It demonstrates a definite relation between the two kinds of experience: the experience of moral accountability and shame effectively precludes the experience of psychological responsibility. The converse is also true.

The inclusion of the subject of the second chapter, "The psychology of self-deception," might at first be puzzling to a reader, but it is easy to explain. Any retreat from the normal experience of autonomy and responsibility for personal action, as in a sincere disclaimer, "I couldn't help it," is in itself a self-deception. The converse holds also: the condition of self-deception is bound to reduce the experience of conviction in what one says or does and the sense of responsibility for it. Consequently, the subject of self-deception figures in almost every other chapter in the book as well as Chapter 2. Most of this chapter deals with self-deception of the comparatively subtle kinds that are defensive or self-protective reactions to the anxiety of internal conflict. The self-deceptions that are central to neurotic conditions are considered here briefly. But there are also more radical and dramatic kinds of self-deception, though generally less chronic, that occur in the face of external threat or coercion. I have included here the phenomena of brainwashing, false confession under police interrogation, political coercion or, sometimes, aggressive therapeutic efforts. I also demonstrate the similarity to these of the effects of personal bullying. The confessions and admissions produced, particularly in situations of terrifying coercion, are striking examples, not merely of submission or telling them what one knows they want to hear, but of a different state of mind in which normal conviction and personal responsibility for what one says has been suspended, or surrendered.

The subject of conviction and responsibility for what one says and believes, or thinks one believes, is continued in Chapter 3, "Two kinds of conscientiousness." I mentioned earlier in this Introduction the place of conscientiousness in obsessive symptoms. Its importance in such symptoms has been recognized since Freud. As we shall see obsessive conscientiousness is not just especially severe or harsh, as is sometimes thought, but is a special kind involving a distinctive mental process. It is a conscientiousness in which the person is under the sway of quasi-external, conscious or semi-conscious, directives or admonitions to himself of the subjective form of "I should" or "I shouldn't." I have called this a conscientiousness of rules, because it is derived from moral precepts such as "I shouldn't waste opportunities," "I should be more generous," etc. whose authority is experienced as superior to one's own inclinations. It is therefore quite distinct from what

I describe as a conscientiousness of conviction that simply expresses one's own values. These two kinds of conscientiousness differ, of course, in the degree of personal responsibility the individual feels for the judgments and actions that follow from each.

In connection with this distinction the chapter considers the subjective quality and, so to speak, the psychological status of moral accountability and the shame that is often associated with it. It considers the relation of these to regular moral convictions or what we call values. That relation is less simple than it may appear to be. An episode in the psychotherapy of a man troubled by a particular moral dilemma is in this instance, too, useful in sharpening the issue. Finally, we consider here the question whether there is any rational place for shame in a world where any action, even the most odious, is in principle psychologically understandable.

I have called Chapter 4 "The self-control muddle" because I think the psychological concept of self-control, as it is used in psychiatry and professional psychology, is indeed muddled. Certain kinds of action, for which personal responsibility is commonly disclaimed are often described in psychiatry and clinical psychology as "failures of impulse control." The description almost invariably refers to impulsive behavior that is considered socially undesirable. It may include aggressive behavior ranging from occasional temper outbursts ("losing it") to violent criminal acts, or it may refer simply to succumbing easily to temptation. All these are thought to be manifestations of an inability to control impulses. They are commonly related by their subjects with a disclaimer of intent or deliberateness such as, "I can't help it" or "I didn't mean it." The latter disclaimer, for instance, is familiar from men who have beaten their wives. These disavowals of responsibility are typically denials of moral culpability, but they are nevertheless often made sincerely. It is the sincerity with which they may be made that has lead, I suspect, to their often being taken at face value even by psychologists and psychiatrists as actual failures of control. As we shall see, however, it is far more likely that such disclaimers of responsibility, however sincere, are also self-deceptions. The notion of a failure or inability to control action implies the unwilling defeat of a desire for control. That premise, usually taken for granted, is very much open to doubt.

The question, in other words, is whether these actions reflect an inability for self-control or a willingness to abandon it, often unrecognized by the one who acts, and by those who observe the action as well. For example, for individuals of a certain sort of personality this kind of sincere disclaimer comes especially easily. These are people whose characteristic way is quick, spur-of-the-moment reaction, action without much deliberate reflection. Action of that sort reduces the time and the self-consciousness of decision, attenuates the process, and makes it comparatively easy to feel "I didn't really mean it." The attenuation of the process of decision also makes it easy to assign responsibility for personal action to its external provocation ("She pushed my buttons"). But this is only one sort of case and does not answer the general question. We shall consider a variety of cases.

The concept of will is considered in Chapter 5 as it is employed in the three ways indicated in the chapter's title, "Will, willpower, free will." In all three ways it carries a suggestion, if not the direct implication, of an independent faculty with an impetus of its own. In this, it is thought separate from, superior to, and at its extreme capable of transcending the regular desires and anxieties that normally motivate action. I think that it is precisely on account of that implication of a capacity to transcend normal motivations and anxieties that the concept has been both attractive and problematic. Perhaps I should say, attractive to some, problematic to others, among whom I include myself. This is especially so in the conceptions of willpower and free will, at least in its stronger sense.

It is of course the idea of free will and the classic philosophical problem of its meaning in a deterministic world of cause and effect that has been, and still is, the most interesting and the most troublesome. This is not a book of philosophy, the usual place for discussion of that subject, but I think that the problem cannot be evaded here. It is clear, after all, that personal responsibility for action has no meaning if personal freedom of choice is an illusion. As a philosophical problem the idea of free will is a subject of logical analysis. The discussion here, however, will be primarily a psychological one. That is, it is informed by psychological observations, specifically observations of certain kinds of subjective experience, in particular the developing experience of free choice, as it occurs in the situation of psychotherapy. It is a well-known claim of psychoanalysis or psychodynamic therapy in general that, if it is successful, the patient's behavior that had been compulsive or automatic, that is, symptomatic behavior, will no longer be compulsive or automatic, but will become a matter of choice. Consideration of this claim is an additional reason for taking up this subject. I have presented in this chapter an episode of psychotherapy that illustrates such a change, thus offering a test of that claim as well as a special view of the reality and the conditions of choice.

Chapters 6 and 7 take up in some detail the self-protective dilution or avoidance of experience of personal responsibility in psychopathology. Some years ago, in a book I called *Neurotic Styles* (1965, 1999), and more recently in my book *Dynamics of Character* (2000), I presented a view of the workings of personality in neurotic conditions that was different from the traditional psychoanalytic picture. It is a formal picture of those conditions. That is, a picture of the ways of thinking and acting, the kinds of emotional experience and the attitudes that are characteristic of the familiar neurotic conditions. I wanted to show that the familiar neurotic symptoms or traits, for instance, obsessive or compulsive symptoms, were actually special expressions of the individual's characteristic attitudes and ways of thinking. This does not mean the attitudes a person might believe were his, but the attitudes, often unrecognized by him, that actually determined how he saw the world and himself. I wanted to show, also, that these characteristic attitudes and ways of thinking—styles, as I called them—are also the ways in which neurotic individuals mitigate or avoid the anxieties of internal conflict. These styles, in other words, fulfilled the self-protective functions that were traditionally assigned in psychoanalysis to the defense mechanisms. In this chapter, I raise the question, and try to answer it, whether an unconsciously self-protective retreat from or dilution of the sense of conviction and responsibility for what one says and does, a retreat in that way from a full expression of oneself as an autonomous being, is common to all neurotic styles. There is, also, the further question whether, in fact, we can understand all the neurotic styles as particular ways in which such a general self-protective aim is achieved. We will have seen in Chapter 2, in a case such as the false confession obtained under police interrogation, that a surrender of personal responsibility and conviction, sincere and unknowing, can be a self-protective reaction to external threat. Is a retreat of that sort from responsibility for personal action and from conviction about what one says or does the fundamental self-protective response to the anxiety of internal conflict as well?

Chapter 7, "Schizophrenia", takes up the kind of psychopathology in which the loss, or surrender, or suspension of autonomous self-direction takes its most radical forms. The chapter considers briefly the question of biological origins of schizophrenia, taking for granted that all psychological capacities and vulnerabilities have origins in genetic variations.

Schizophrenia, we presume, reflects such a vulnerability. It is widely agreed at present that the central feature of schizophrenic symptomatology is its cognitive problem of thought disorder. And there is much evidence, some of which will be cited in the chapter, that some loss or failure of autonomous, volitional direction of thought and attention is critical to this thought disorder. It is manifest in various well-known schizophrenic symptoms such as "looseness" of associative connections, "cognitive slippage," or tangentiality of thinking. It will be possible, in light of the far less severe, but self-protective surrender of autonomous thinking in neurotic conditions, to offer some conjecture concerning such a self-protective function of the schizophrenic retreat from autonomy as well. It is not necessary to assume that the specific schizophrenic symptoms are themselves self-protective. It is more likely that a self-protective or defensive retreat from autonomy in cognitive function may lead to those radical symptoms.

Chapter 8, "Saying something is doing something," takes up a problem that appears in psychoanalytic and psychoanalytically influenced psychotherapy, but also has important implications for the understanding of human behavior in general. The therapeutic issue concerns the tendency in psychoanalytic treatment, inherited from its earliest history, to consider the ideational content of the patients' productions, that is, what the patient says, as the "therapeutic material," without sufficient regard for the attitude with which that content is produced. The conception, argued against here, is of speech as given impetus by, and the product of, needs, wishes or thoughts. Opposed to that view, is the understanding of speech as employed by a person for a purpose, as purposeful action: saying something is doing something. One common result of the former tendency in psychoanalysis and psychotherapy is the patient's achievement of what is called intellectual insight without significant personal change. The early, psychoanalytical, work of Wilhelm Reich was important in identifying this problem and I shall cite some of his observations and corrective precepts. Several clinical examples are provided to illustrate how saying something is doing something, although not always as clearly and wholeheartedly as the speaker intends. The larger problem involved here is the view of behavior in general as the product of forces and agencies moving the person, to the neglect of the processes of conscious self-direction. It is a conception of behavior that neglects and, for its subject, dilutes, the experience of responsibility for, or ownership of, what the person says or does.

Chapter 9 takes us in a different direction. The retreat from autonomy and the experience of responsibility that have been discussed in previous chapters are largely involuntary and unconscious processes. In Chapter 9, "Voluntary surrender of responsibility," however, we look at situations in which surrender of autonomy and responsibility and the mental state associated with such surrender are sought quite consciously and deliberately, even eagerly. These are cases of conscious, even radical, surrender of responsibility to charismatic leaders or movements, not only for what is said and done, but also for what is believed. We will consider two charismatic religious groups, Rev. Sun Myung Moon's Unification Church and the International Society for Krishna Consciousness (ISKON), with special interest in the subjective and cognitive state that seems an essential condition for their practices. In addition, we will take a look at other settings, including the radical Islamic movement, in which individual autonomy and personal responsibility are surrendered.

Finally, let me add a word about the point of view and the nature of the experience that have informed this book and are responsible for the interests it reflects. I am a clinician, a psychotherapist with a background in psychoanalysis. That is the source of my interest in subjective life, especially subjective life that is not consciously articulated and is largely unrecognized by the one who lives it. This is a level of mentation that is not quite identical with what is usually understood as the psychoanalytic unconscious. It is a level of thought and feeling that, while not consciously recognized by its subject, invariably shows itself in the expression in their eyes and the tone of their speech as well as, often, what they say. As I have indicated in this Introduction, I have in most chapters offered instances, much condensed excerpts, of exchanges with patients in psychotherapy, conducted both by me and others, to clarify and illustrate aspects of subjective experience relevant to the subjects at hand. I believe that the intimacy of the therapeutic situation offers a unique access to that experience. Even though the individuals, disguised of course, who appear in these exchanges were patients in psychotherapy, their experience, though possibly more acute at the time, will be essentially familiar to everyone. The therapeutic material is not offered to illustrate or suggest a particular therapeutic method, but only for the purpose I have indicated.

References

Kaiser, H. (1955) The problem of responsibility in psychotherapy. *Psychiatry, 18,* 205–211; also in L. B. Fierman (Ed.) (1965) *Effective psychotherapy: the contribution of Hellmuth Kaiser.* New York: Free Press.

Shapiro, D. (1965, 1999) *Neurotic styles.* New York: Basic Books.

Shapiro, D. (2000) *Dynamics of character.* New York: Basic Books.

Chapter 1

Two kinds of responsibility

It is best to begin by sharpening the meaning of the kind of responsibility for personal action that this book is mainly concerned with. That requires clarifying the distinction between two kinds of responsibility, both of them familiar. It happens that the meaning of these two kinds of responsibility and the distinction between them shows itself very clearly in connection with the experience of certain patients in psychotherapy. Let me explain.

People who constantly reproach themselves for mistakes or lapses of one kind or another are usually considered to have an excessive sense of personal responsibility. They feel responsible even for failures or mistakes that are obviously beyond their capacity to avoid. It is generally the aim of psychotherapy to diminish such self-reproach and the exaggerated sense of responsibility it seems to be founded on. Yet psychotherapy is also thought to have a contrary aim. If it is successful, it is supposed to increase the patient's experience of authorship or responsibility for what he or she does (Kaiser 1955; Shapiro 1989). That expectation for psychotherapy of an increased or enlarged responsibility for personal action refers to the fact that neurotic patients invariably show some degree of estrangement from what they do or feel. They regularly say in psychotherapy that they do things they really don't want to do, that they continue relationships they get nothing out of, that they somehow don't do what they're sure they actually want to do; or, they feel, and say, that their actions are governed not by their own wishes, but by others' expectations, or by established routine. That is what, for example, one such person had in mind when he likened the way he lived to a train running along a track that has been laid down. As I said in the Introduction, the innovative psychoanalyst Hellmuth Kaiser (1955) was the first to take note of this diminished sense of responsibility, observing it as it appeared in his patients' speech. He said that they often did not seem to be completely "behind" what they were saying. Their expression of emotion was often forced. They often seemed to lack conviction about what they were saying. These are all reflections of a certain estrangement from the self; it is the sort of thing we psychologists or psychoanalysts mean when we say that the neurotic personality is not well integrated. If psychotherapy is successful, it is said to diminish that kind of self-estrangement, to achieve a greater integration of the personality, so that the individual knows more clearly what he or she wants, and wants to do, in that sense feels more fully represented by it and takes a stronger sense of responsibility for it.

It is evident, then, that there are two different meanings or kinds of responsibility here—the kind that therapy aims to diminish and the kind it aims to enlarge—and two different kinds of subjective experience. The kind of responsibility contained in self-reproach can be called the moral sense of responsibility and for convenience I will call its alternative the psychological sense of responsibility. The moral kind of responsibility refers to an individual's duty or obligation ("It's Johnny's responsibility to take care of that") and the person is morally accountable. Someone who is reliable in fulfilling moral obligations we call a responsible person. A failure of responsibility of this kind is likely to elicit reproach, sometimes from others and often from the individuals themselves. If it is a serious matter, this will likely include shame, being shamed or shaming oneself. The psychological kind of responsibility, on the other hand, has a meaning quite separate from moral responsibility. It refers simply to the authorship or cause or source of the action ("Robert Moses was responsible for building that bridge"). It can refer to the action of someone else or of course to one's own action. Objectively, this kind of responsibility is simply a factual matter. But our interest here is in the subjective experience of responsibility, what one might call the person's attitude toward his own action and its result. That attitude would normally include the sense that what one is doing or has done is what he has wanted or chosen to do. It is a sense, at least a tacit sense, of agency or personal autonomy. But as we shall see, though agency and personal autonomy are objective facts of human action, they are by no means invariably the individual's subjective experience. The sense of having chosen and intended to do what one has done, the sense of responsibility for it, can be diluted or distorted in many ways, or even be absent altogether.

These two kinds of responsibility are certainly different, but they are not entirely different. The reality of volition and personal choice is central to both ideas of responsibility, but their conceptions of volition and choice are quite different. One is concerned with the moral judgment of choice and personal action, while the other is concerned with the understanding of its reasons. But they are not only different. There is also a definite relation between the two kinds of experience of responsibility, actually a dynamic relation. They are in conflict with one another. To the extent that the one kind of experience of responsibility predominates, the other kind is diminished or even extinguished. To the extent that the person has a sense of his action as an understandable expression of his state of mind or point of view at the time, moral judgment of the action, as in self-reproach, is weakened. Conversely, to the extent that the experience of moral responsibility and, specifically, self-reproach are strong, the experience of an action as an understandable choice is precluded. This exclusionary relation between the moral and psychological kinds of responsibility exists not only in the subjective life of the individual himself; it holds also in any consideration of others' behavior. We see that, for instance, in considering criminal behavior. Moral reproach obstructs empathic understanding; empathic understanding weakens moral reproach. I want now to look more closely at these two kinds of responsibility, the subjective experience of each, and their relationship. We will then see that relationship demonstrated in a particular case of self-reproach, as it undergoes a change in a therapeutic setting.

Self-reproach is punishment for having done or not done something. Its message is: I shouldn't (or should) have done that. But self-reproach is not merely regret, and its aim is not simply correction; correction would be superfluous where the one to be corrected is also the one who corrects. The aim of self-reproach, as I said, is punishment and, consistent with that aim, its tone is aggressive; it is often accompanied by explicit denunciation ("I shouldn't have run away! I'm a coward!"). Like most accusations and charges aimed at punishment, self-reproach is likely to exaggerate transgressions. It is a corollary of that exaggeration that the person who reproaches himself usually does not believe all of the accusations he makes against himself. His aim, after all, is not to consider the facts, but to inflict pain. But the accusations and the repentant admission ("I shouldn't have done that") do constitute an acceptance of moral responsibility.

The premise of self-reproach is not only that one should or shouldn't have done something but, also, that one might at that moment have chosen to do otherwise. That premise—we shall discuss it at greater length later in Chapter 5—presents a problem not just for philosophers, as it has, but, in a way that is special, for psychoanalysts and psychotherapists. For psychoanalysts and psychotherapists are accustomed to assuming that what their patients have done had its reasons in the point of view and the circumstances of the ones who did it, whether they were clearly conscious of those reasons or not, and that those reasons were decisive. This is more than a logical assumption; it reflects a certain interest and an attitude. It is fundamental to any therapeutic method interested in understanding, as opposed to correcting, behavior. It is for that matter fundamental to understanding any behavior, whether in the psychologist's office, the court room, or the friend's kitchen table. The attitude of self-reproach, however, and for that matter the attitude of moral reproach in general, whether directed at oneself or others, is not friendly to an empathic understanding of a transgressor's point of view. It is not well disposed toward an interest in the circumstances, as they seemed to him, that might account for his transgression. The one who reproaches himself, or someone else, is not interested in reasons or psychology. Those reasons and that psychology are irrelevant to the assignment of moral responsibility.

The focus of moral reproach is the evaluation of the act itself, the transgression. The act is evaluated according to some principle or personal ideal (bravery, generosity, perhaps what an admired or imagined figure would have done). Such general principles or ideals define what should have been done, and, it is presumed, might have been done by anyone. Only in certain exceptional cases of obvious incapacity might this presumption be overlooked. It is this presumption that any choice is available to anyone that justifies moral evaluation and, specifically, self-reproach and the punishment, the shame, it entails.

Actually, of course, an empathic understanding of the transgressor's reasons and point of view is not only irrelevant to the assignment of moral responsibility and the attitude of reproach or self-reproach. It weakens and undermines them. Understanding evokes sympathy. The maxim is: to understand is to forgive, even ourselves. Understanding empathically the point of view of the one who acts ultimately makes his action seem necessary or even, at least as it seemed to him, reasonable. That is to say, necessary and reasonable for this person, at that time, in those circumstances. Not perhaps for someone else, even in the same circumstances, but with a different point of view, but for him. In effect, an empathic understanding recognizes that this act by this person in these circumstances was inevitable. This does not mean that this person had no choice. It means, rather, that the choice that he made, from among the possibilities that were defined by his point of view, was bound to seem to him the one to make.

But while it is true that a recognition of the limitations and tendencies of an individual's point of view weakens self-reproach and undermines the basis of moral responsibility or accountability, it is also true that it expands an experience of responsibility of a different kind. It sharpens the person's awareness that he chose to do what he did, that he chose to do it for his own reasons, reasons that can be understood, that what he did promised some kind of satisfaction or, if not satisfaction, at least some relief from what was no longer bearable, or, if neither of those, then the escape, however costly, from some prospect that threatened to be even costlier. In short, that what one did made sense, at that time, from the standpoint of this person. Thus the weakening of one kind of experience of responsibility is at the same stroke the strengthening of the experience of the other kind. This new sense of responsibility consists of the awareness that what was done was not a failure of one's will, but an expression of one's will, not a lapse of judgment, but an exercise of judgment, not an act that was "against my aims and values," but only against what I imagined my aims and values to be, not "unlike me" at all, unlike only my image of myself.

It is the realization, for example, by the young woman who thinks that she wants to get out of a troubled relationship, but somehow "can't," that she only thinks she *should* leave, but doesn't want to. Or the husband's realization that it is not, as he thought, that he just "lost it" and "didn't really mean to hurt" his wife, but rather that his manly pride had been wounded and its repair required that he "teach her a lesson." Or even the realization, by the man who says he "can't shake" the terrible obsessive thought that he might rape his daughter, that he has, without realizing it, been afraid of *not* examining his mind for that very thought, believing that if such a thought exists without his awareness, he might actually lose control and do it. Each of these initial disclaimers of responsibility, though sincere, will, as spoken, have lacked confidence or complete conviction. Each of these realizations constitutes an increased consciousness of purpose and intention, of agency, or responsibility for one's action. Inasmuch as each diminishes the person's estrangement from himself, each can also be said to constitute an increased integration of the personality. As each clarifies that what was done was expressive of a particular person's point of view at that moment in those particular circumstances, and the compelling aims that followed from it, each shows the reproachful, "I shouldn't have done it! I should have done something else!" to be, in its logical implication, equivalent to the fanciful, "I should have *been* someone else."

Let me illustrate the two kinds of responsibility and their relation to each other with a specific example. I will do that with a much-condensed presentation of a therapeutic change consisting of the relief of severe self-reproach, as it occurred in the course of psychotherapy with a particular person. Identifying details have of course been altered. The material in this presentation does not require any special interest in or familiarity with psychotherapy as such and its aim is not to demonstrate a therapeutic method.

The patient was a 41-year-old married woman, a successful, accomplished, extremely ambitious university professor. She had been severely depressed for about 2 months, since shortly after the birth of her first child. Her condition had been diagnosed as postpartum depression. She had delivered her baby, a girl, without unusual difficulty and initially had seemed happy. She had looked forward to the birth with great hopefulness, especially as she felt it was, in view of her age, her "last chance." But she became noticeably depressed about 2 weeks after the birth and shortly afterward attempted suicide. Since that time, she had refused to have anything to do with the care of the baby. She had been hospitalized after the suicide attempt, medicated, had apparently improved and been discharged. But when she returned home she immediately reverted to her earlier condition. She refused further medication. The care of the baby was turned over to her husband and an elderly housekeeper who moved into the house for that purpose. The patient was described by her husband as sitting silently at home all day, saying little or nothing, eating little, occasionally crying silently. When asked to perform some caretaking act for the baby, her response invariably was a quiet "I can't." She began psychotherapy at the insistence of her husband. I will describe several exchanges between the patient and the therapist.

In the initial session and for several weeks thereafter, she sat silently, just as she had been described. The therapist's occasional comments elicited very little response or none at all. Several times she did refer to her husband, always in the same way:

Patient: He's so fine . . . and Emily (the housekeeper-caretaker) too . . . they're doing everything. . . . God knows how he's doing his job, too . . . but he does it, he does his job.
Therapist: You mean in contrast to you.
Patient: What I've put them through, hell.
Therapist: I suppose you've all been through hell, including you.
Patient: But it's my fault!
Therapist: That you feel the way you do?
Patient: Don't you believe that people are responsible for themselves!
Therapist: For the way they feel? No, I don't think you have any choice about that.

She sat silently, seeming to be concentrating, as though working on something.

Therapist: You are silent, but you certainly don't look peaceful.
Patient: Susie (her baby) is damaged. She's damaged already. I know it!
Therapist: Damaged? How?
Patient: (impatiently, insistently, but vaguely and without conviction) She's not developing as fast as she should. I know it!

This woman's insistence that her child was in some unspecified way "damaged" exemplifies the punishing aim of self-reproach. Her emphatic and repeated assertions of certainty of this damage ("I know it!") were not expressions of conviction. They were punishing accusations against herself, magnifying her culpability with the exaggeration and force common, not to genuine conviction, but to the wish to punish. The therapist responds:

Therapist: You don't sound much convinced of this "damage."
Patient: I just think to myself, over and over, that she's been damaged and that it's too late to make up. . . . When I sit home, I think that over and over . . . that's what I think all day.
Therapist: That isn't just "thinking." It's accusing. I suppose that's what you do all day, as you say, accuse yourself "over and over."

Patient: (defensively) I can't take care of her! I just can't!
Therapist: OK, if you can't, you can't, but you say it as if you're in a courtroom answering a charge.

Some time later the patient made the accusation against herself in a different form.

Patient: (aggressively) I've failed in the basic function of a woman.

This cliché, inconsistent with her general style, was, again, an exaggeration, said without conviction.

Therapist: That's what women are good for? That's how they should be measured? I don't think you believe it.
Patient: (angrily) You're just trying to make me feel better! But how can I forget it, what I've done, what I'm still doing! I can't forget it!
Therapist: When you say you "can't" forget it, do you mean, perhaps, that you can't allow yourself to forget it, that you shouldn't forget it, that it would be wrong to relent?

She did not respond directly to this, but seemed to soften, to relax a bit. Shortly afterward, she spoke for the first time of what preceded the present crisis, starting with her pregnancy, and anticipation of the baby:

Patient: I studied very hard for it.

She explained that she had read extensively over a period of months on the psychology of infancy and was well into the psychoanalytic literature on the subject. She had also gone through an extensive course on natural childbirth. All this work and studying, she said ironically, was in preparation for her "big success" as a mother. The therapist said (incorrectly, as it turned out):

I suppose you were nervous about it, wanted to reassure yourself.
Patient: (crying, for the first time) No, I don't think I was nervous about it. In fact, I felt self-confident. I knew the material.

She explained that after the birth at first she was very happy. But then, after the baby was home for a few days, she was very tense. Things didn't go well. Nothing went according to expectations, according to the books and professional advice. She was frightened. There were no relatives to turn to. Her own mother, no longer living, had been a businesslike, detached person. She was the younger child, separated from an older brother by several years. She always had been a good student, studied hard, and in adolescence became an outstanding student. Grades had meant a great deal to her.

At this point she remembered that once before in her life she had gotten "terribly panicky." She explained that when she was about to complete her graduate work she had applied for a position at a different institution from her present one and was about to give the customary job talk there based on her research. Several days before the scheduled talk, her advisor had raised a technical question that she had in fact answered adequately. However, afterward she became extremely worried about whether she would do well in the talk itself. On the day before the scheduled presentation she became panicky, decided that she "simply couldn't" go through with it, cancelled the talk and withdrew her application.

Therapist: When you say that you "couldn't" go through with it, I assume you mean that you were afraid to risk not doing well and wouldn't go through with it.
Patient: (impatiently, as if that should be obvious) Well, of course.

The resemblance of this incident to her current situation—her fear of doing what she might not do well or with outstanding success, and the shame and humiliation that would entail—was not lost on her.

We see here a change in this person's attitude toward her own action, a change initially represented in her recollection of an earlier action when she was faced with an anxiety similar to the present one. Her experience, first recalled as *I couldn't* do it, was now recognized by her as *I wouldn't* do it. This enlargement of subjective experience is critical. One might even conjecture that the experience of the active *"wouldn't,"* in contrast to the helpless *"couldn't,"* may have contained some consciousness of the reasons, the anxieties that prompted her refusal. Altogether, the transformation from a sense of *I couldn't* (or, in the present situation, *I can't*), as though helplessly and unwillingly disabled, to an awareness of an intentional, even, from her standpoint, reasoned, refusal can be described as an enlargement of her experience of personal responsibility for her action. Perhaps it could be described, also, as a raising of the volitional level of her action, in the specific sense of its increased consciousness of intentionality or deliberateness.

This enlargement of her sense of responsibility for her action, of the reality of her refusal and the reason for it, corresponded with the articulation and the weakening of her self-reproach. Her initial attitude of self-reproach obstructed an understanding of the reasons for her action and its intention, and therefore a full experience of psychological responsibility for it. One could say, in fact, that her punitive point of view made it *impermissible* for her to turn her attention to an empathic understanding of her reasons. This moralistic attitude was in fact expressed in her angry, even indignant, reaction to the therapist's more understanding attitude ("You're just trying to make me feel better!"). It was only as that attitude of moral responsibility, initially rather haughty in its way, softened that it became possible—actually, permissible—for her to turn her attention to a different view of her action. It was then that she was able to "remember" reasons for her comparable action in earlier, comparable, circumstances.

Some further points concerning the enlargement of this person's experience of responsibility for her action are worth noting. Her psychological change was associated with a certain kind of physical or vocal change. Her voice and manner of speaking became more conversational and the somewhat forced and exaggerated manner of her expressions of self-reproach noticeably diminished. She emerged as a more genuine person; it could almost be said that she became more herself. From a somewhat abstract psychological standpoint the newly enlarged experience of responsibility for her action signaled a greater unity or integration of her personality. This means, subjectively, that she felt more at one with what she did. The change in her experience of herself, will have a further consequence in a change of her experience of her child. Initially her relation to and image of her child were largely products of her reproaches of herself. Her exaggerated concerns about her child ("She's damaged, I know it") were punitive reminders of her own failure. The relaxation of this self-imposed punishment therefore has a dual result in subjective experience: the strain of that self-conscious effort is removed and she speaks, as I said, with a more relaxed voice; at the same time, her idea of her child, is freed of that influence. A clearer sense of herself and a more objective picture of her baby emerge together from the tendentious fusion of the two.

References

Kaiser, H. (1955) The problem of responsibility in psychotherapy. *Psychiatry, 18*, 205–211; also in *Effective psychotherapy: the contribution of Hellmuth Kaiser* (1965) ed. Fierman, L. B. New York: Free Press.

Shapiro, D. (1989) *Psychotherapy of neurotic character.* New York: Basic Books.

Chapter 2

The psychology of self-deception

Let me first recall this subject's relation, mentioned in the Introduction, to the other subjects in this book and to our general interest. Objectively speaking, adult humans are autonomous, self-directing creatures. It follows from this that all the ways in which people avoid or dilute or surrender their experience of autonomy and responsibility for their action are exercises of self-deception. The converse is also true: self-deception invariably weakens the experience of responsibility for personal action. Self-deceptive speech or action cannot be wholehearted; it never achieves conviction. In that sense, the effort to deceive oneself is never completely successful. The one who deceives himself may say what he has to say loudly or repeatedly or with exaggerated emphasis, but he is never completely committed to it. Self-deception and a weakened experience of responsibility for what one says are inseparable.

In some ways the psychology of self-deception has been obscure and it is easy to lose one's way in it. It is best to start with an example. Let me give an instance in which it seems that believing, or knowing, something is not as simple and unambiguous a condition as one might imagine. A businessman is talking about his partner and friend of many years. He chooses his words carefully. Hesitantly and with obvious reluctance, he says that "it is possible" that this man has been cheating him. He is silent for a moment, then he says, quietly, that he thinks he has known this "in a way" for a long time. Finally, after pausing, he adds, "But you don't really know it until you say it out loud."

So we see that there are two kinds or levels of knowing: knowing "in a way" and "really" knowing. Furthermore, the elevation from one to the other is brought about, at least in this case, by "saying it out loud." The conversion, in other words, is not a matter of acquiring additional information, but of conscious articulation of what was already in some sense known, but not articulated. One might call it a process of consciousness raising. The earlier state was one in which the speaker did not know (and clearly did not want to know) what he knew; the final state was one in which he realized what he knew, admitting it to his listener and to himself at the same time. The distinction here is between what one thinks or believes about something and what one imagines oneself to think or believe.[1] A disjunction between these two is what we mean by self-deception.

The idea of self-deception can easily seem paradoxical. How can the deceiver, who must know what is not to be known, also be the unknowing deceived? How can one intentionally, knowingly, not know? The process clearly requires a selective monitoring of one's own thoughts. It is that process of self-selection that is sometimes taken to imply both knowing what must not be known and at the same time being able to not know it. It is true that psychoanalysis offers a comparatively easy solution. But the psychoanalytic solution, at least in its traditional form, requires the assumption of an independent unconscious agency, the ego, which can intentionally deceive the conscious person, a "smart" unconscious. In this way, the problem of separating the deceiver from the deceived is accomplished, but only by reifying a descriptive concept.

Certainly self-deception implies a self-monitoring process of some sort. But the assumption that this monitoring process must be smart, or knowing, is altogether unnecessary. A selective monitoring of one's mind and even the self-regulation of certain action coordinated with monitoring does not necessarily require intelligent understanding. We jerk our hand away from the hot plate not because we are afraid of damage to the skin, but because it hurts. In other words, for the process of self-deception it is not necessary to know what we must not know; it is only necessary for the presence of something that we must not know to be signaled in some way while it is still in incipient form. This kind of regulatory system is well known to dynamic psychology and such a system does in fact exist; it involves the individual's personality and attitudes. According to a person's makeup he will experience some form of discomfort at the incipient presence of an idea or feeling that is inimical to his attitudes and therefore threatens his psychological stability. It is not necessary for him to know, and in fact for the most part we do not know, the nature of the immediate threat, in order to react to it, according to our individual ways, to relieve or mitigate its discomfort. The personality in this way works as a monitoring and signaling system.

The process of self-deception, of course, must include not only a system of signaling a threatening idea but, also, action to forestall or mitigate that threat. It must include a way of forestalling consciousness of inimical ideas or feelings, and it must do so, not without the individual's mental activity, but without his full awareness. According to his makeup or personality organization the individual possesses capabilities of this kind as well. It is not only that one reacts with discomfort to the vague sensation of inimical ideas or feelings. That discomfort in turn prompts certain mental activity, perhaps including the mobilizing of reassuring or disapproving thoughts, that forestalls further conscious articulation of those inimical ideas or feelings. We will consider these processes and the nature of that activity later in some detail. For the time being, it is enough to say that it is the individual's personality and the attitudes to which these ideas or feelings are inimical and discomforting, that prompt him to thought-action that prevents their further conscious development. The monitoring and the corrective systems therefore are one. The thought activity comprising monitoring and correction together constitutes a psychological stabilizing process. But that process has a psychological cost. It results in a rift between what the person believes and what he tells himself and thinks he believes.

For example, consider the businessman I cited before. Vague suspicions of his partner that arose earlier must have been disturbing to him, perhaps even before they were recognized for what they were. The discomforting sensation of, say, his own disloyalty to his old friend might in turn prompt a loyal assembling of contrary evidence and reassuring ideas. These, in turn, might obviate for the time being further conscious development and articulation of his suspicions. But the result of a quick and essentially reflexive process such as this can only be a continuing effort and a rift between what he believes, perhaps even what his eyes tell him, and what he tells himself that he believes.

Even if self-deception is not particularly paradoxical, it has to be said that it is a strange human capability in a way that the ability to lie to another person is not. Deceiving someone else is clearly advantageous in certain situations, sometimes even essential, but self-deception does not seem so at all. From an evolutionary standpoint, it is hard to see any adaptive advantage to the capability for it. On the contrary, we count the existence of reasonably trustworthy judgment and feelings about reality as indispensable to our survival. Yet here we are confronted with the fact that a person's best judgment or genuine assessment of reality can be overruled by that person himself. This is no rare or even unusual phenomenon; it is apparently a universal susceptibility. I believe the answer is indicated in the dynamics I have just described. Under certain psychological circumstances, self-deception can dispel or mitigate discomfort, even if it creates a lesser one, and in that way it is a stabilizing process and self-protective. It may be useful in its immediate and particular effect even if it is maladaptive as a general phenomenon. There is a certain support for this view in the fact that it appears to be a regular and lasting, even characteristic, feature of all neurotic conditions and in fact central to their workings.

I have referred in the Introduction to the exceedingly interesting clinical observation made by Hellmuth Kaiser (1955) of a particular quality in the manner of speech he found regularly in his patients. Kaiser, it is interesting to note, had been a student of Wilhelm Reich in the early days when Reich, in his work on character analysis emphasized the importance of patients' ways of saying what they said. Kaiser said that his patients "do not talk straight." He explained that although they were perfectly sincere, their speech seemed without exception to give the impression of some artificiality. What they said did not seem to express what they actually thought or felt. The tears sometimes seemed forced or worked up; the story of childhood sounded rehearsed; the angry account of yesterday's event, as one listened to it, had the quality of a public oration. It was artificial, but there was no suggestion of a conscious intention to deceive the listener. It was in this quality of speech that Kaiser recognized the speaker's absence of conviction or of a sense of full responsibility for what he said. What Kaiser observed, though he did not describe it this way, was self-deceptive speech.

This kind of speech is obviously not limited to patients in psychotherapy. It is fairly common in everyday discourse. It is the sort of thing that people have noticed when they say about someone, "She is theatrical" or "He's so pompous" or, more specifically, "He is trying to convince himself." As a matter of fact, it is the sort of observation that anyone, with sufficient interest and perhaps a little training, can easily make here and there in ordinary social discourse. It is clear in these observations that self-deception is an action, a speech action, and at least part of its process, not only its result, is objectively observable. The individual is doing something, however unwittingly. It is not therefore a strictly internal process. Nor is it, as such self-protective processes are generally considered to be in psychoanalysis, entirely unconscious. Although it obviously is not consciously and deliberately planned, it clearly involves not only some degree of conscious, though unwitting, activity, but even conscious effort in thought and speech.

Self-deceptive speech is unusual in several respects. Above all, it does not have the communicative aims one ordinarily assumes speech to have. Its aim is not so much to communicate with the listener as to affect the speaker himself. That is, it is typically aimed at mitigating or dispelling some anxiety or discomfort of the speaker's. For example, a man who has just made a difficult decision tries, with a conspicuous lack of success in this instance, to dispel his doubts about what he has done. He says emphatically and with an unusually loud voice, "I know I did the right thing! ... (more quietly) I think." The exaggerated emphasis in this example, specifically the emphatic assertion of conviction and confidence is characteristic of this kind of speech. Frequently, repetitions of an assertion ("I know I did the right thing! I know I did!") serve the same purpose.

One can sometimes see a similar self-deceptive effort in forced or melodramatic expressions of emotion or similarly self-conscious descriptions of emotional states. Thus, a young man speaks of being "furious" after an unpleasant exchange with his difficult father ("I hate my father!"), but, despite his apparent efforts, he doesn't look furious. He later "admits" that actually he feels sorry for his father, but dislikes himself for being "so soft." In all these cases, one has the impression of an effort being made in the utterance itself. These speakers are sincere; they imagine that they do feel what they are trying to feel, most often what they think they should feel. It is acting, but of a special sort. It is acting in which the actor is his own audience. The speaker's attention is much more on what he is doing than on the listener. It seems that the self-deception actually receives its final construction in the act of speech. The speech is not merely the vehicle for an already unconsciously composed effort. Perhaps all self-deception is finally constructed in speech, either silently to oneself or with an external listener; certainly it seems true for a large class. It would not be remarkable if this were so. If, as seems the case, a genuine feeling or belief achieves its fully conscious form in speech, particularly in "saying it out loud," the same might be expected of self-deception.

There is another characteristic of this kind of speech, noticeable to the listener, which confirms its essentially noncommunicative nature. When a speaker says, "I know I did the right thing!" or "I hate my father!" or some such, with an exaggerated emphasis, the listener does not have a sense of being addressed. The speaker's voice is often louder than his normal conversational voice, the voice that is used to communicate with another person. Further, he does not seem to be looking at the listener in the ordinary way. The listener does not seem to be in his focus; he seems to be looking past him. The attention of the one who speaks this way is inward, in the way of someone listening to himself. He is talking like a person who is quite alone, practicing a speech. In some instances this inwardness has an expression which at first does not seem inward at all. Sometimes the speaker looks directly and searchingly at the listener's eyes. The response he sees, or thinks he sees, in the listener's eyes has a special importance to him; he is remarkably sensitive to it. A confirming response produces visible relief, while the slightest hesitation is quite discomforting and often prompts the speaker to renewed efforts. It seems, however, despite his apparent concentration on the listener, that here, too, the speaker is actually addressing and listening to himself. His concentration on the listener's expression is misleading; he is watching the listener in the way one looks intensely in the mirror for signs of a sore or shaving nick, losing awareness of the mirror itself. His attention is focused on himself. He is addressing and listening to himself through the listener. In doing psychotherapy, I have sometimes half-seriously waved my hand to catch the patient's attention when he is, though seated facing me only a few feet away, speaking this way and clearly not talking to me or really seeing me. The effect is striking; the speaker is startled for a moment, then laughs at himself, at his preoccupation with himself.

Altogether, in self-deceptive speech, the speaker has lost the normal awareness of the listener as an independent, external figure. He has lost the normal "polarity" between them, as the psychologist Heinz Werner (1948) called it, the awareness of the separate existence of speaker and listener. This is sometimes confirmed, as I said, when one happens to interrupt the speaker and he reacts with an embarrassed laugh. It is not only that at that moment he becomes more conscious of the listener's presence. He also becomes aware of himself as an independent figure as well, as someone who is doing something. The full experience of his action is at that moment restored.

To tell oneself, however insistently, that one does not see what is there is one thing, to actually persuade oneself of that is another. It speaks for a special relationship not only with oneself but, also, with reality. It is a common idea that a loss of reality, of a more or less objective sense of the world, is a defining symptom of psychosis, distinguishing psychosis from neurotic conditions and certainly from normality. But it is not quite so. For instance, a dogmatic person, quite nonpsychotic, but whose schematic observations are oblivious of what is new or unexpected, has surely lost something of the normal experience of external reality. Similarly, a suggestible person, whose ideas change from one moment to another according to surrounding opinion, must be said to have a fainter sense of objective reality than most. The dogmatic person has, one might say, overruled the normal more or less objective cognitive attitude of looking things over and seeing how they look in favor of forcibly constructing a picture that conforms with some principled expectation. Similarly, the suggestible person suspends the normal consideration of how things look in favor, say, of an easy satisfaction with how they are commonly said to look. In both these cases a prior internal anxiety has compromised and inhibited the normal interest in, or relation to, external reality in favor of one that is less anxious or more comfortable to them. In this process, personal independent judgment has in some measure unwittingly been suspended and, though it may not be articulated, genuine conviction has been replaced by experience something like "it must be . . ." in the one case, or "everybody says . . ." in the other.

Such a suspension of objective interest in external reality is not a fixed and stable condition, existing without tension and effort. Notwithstanding what one may think one feels and believes about something, what one actually feels and believes remains at the edge of awareness. Sometimes it spontaneously intrudes into awareness ("I know I did the right thing. . . . I think"). It is in that sense that self-deception is never completely successful. That is why self-deceptive remarks are often repeated ("I'm sure of it! I'm absolutely sure of it!") and why they are marked by artificiality and a special insistence and exaggeration. That, also, is why self-deceptive statements are not reliable predictors of action. It is well-known, for instance, that dutiful people by no means actually do all that they insistently say, and sincerely think, they want to do. For example, a recently divorced woman reproaches herself severely for failing to make arrangements for a trip she insists she "really wants" to take. She blames her inaction on "inertia." Shortly, however, she relaxes somewhat. She then says something quite different about her plan, that "it would be good for me." Finally, more quietly, she says that actually she hates to travel alone and knows no one where she had planned to go. This last, she says as if she means it.

It is worth noting here, also, as I have in the previous discussion, that the emergence of the individual's genuine feelings from a state of self-deception is inseparable from the simultaneous emergence of a more objective picture of the external object of those feelings. This person's initial idea of her plan was a product of her effort to persuade herself of its desirability. As that effort to believe something that she did not believe relaxes, she is able to picture her plan as she really saw it. The experience of conviction returns and a clearer sense of herself and of the external world emerges out of the fusion of both.

Another familiar kind of self-deception is a slight variation of the one just cited. In the former case, the individual imagines that she wants to do something, but fails to do it; it is just as common that people think they do not want to do what in fact they do, often regularly. People often say that they eat or drink "more than (they) want to" or lose their temper and say things they "did not mean." They often continue relationships while insisting that they really want to end them. In these cases, also, the relaxation or dissolving of the self-deception—as may happen, for example, in the course of psychotherapy—has a dual result. The recovery of the individual's genuine feelings—that in fact they do not want to end the relationship, but only think they should—is accompanied by the emergence of a clearer picture of the object of those feelings. The man who disapproves of his relationship and thinks he wants to end it begins to recognize the reasons he does not do so. At the same time that he becomes aware of his own feelings, his picture of the object of those feelings becomes more clear. A sense of himself, on the one hand, and of the external figure, on the other, emerges from a vague, anxiety-driven and prejudiced construction that had mainly expressed his disapproval of himself.

Self-deceptive statements and constructions are not judgments of reality, though they pretend to be; they are actions performed on the self and done for their effect on the self. Sometimes this is made clear in a particularly obvious way: a man who is involved in a difficult contest declares loudly and with a transparent effort at conviction, "I'm going to win! I know it!" The listener remarks that he sounds more determined than convinced. The man is surprised, initially displeased, but then amused at himself. He says, now in a different voice, "I say it to myself all day. Like a mantra." A mantra is no false belief. It is something altogether different, a different kind of thinking, from belief. Like an incantation, it has a relation to reality that is different from that of belief or conviction. It is therefore not remarkable that the two, mantra and belief, can exist in the same mind; but not side by side, not both accessible to awareness at the same time.

The kind of self-deception and self-deceptive speech I have considered so far is driven by anxieties of internal origin. The content of the self-deception is determined by the nature of those anxieties or, rather, the nature of the effort to dispel them. The not-quite-believed effort to reassure oneself is prompted by the not-quite-articulated anxious doubt. But there is also a kind of self-deception that is a product of external threat or coercion. The confessions produced by Chinese thought reform practices or Soviet-style show-trials; the supposed recovery of doubtful traumatic memories at therapeutic insistence, or the equally doubtful remembering, under duress, of criminal acts never committed. All those are products of coercion that is more or less impersonal, but there are also cases closer to home. One sort, not rare, is the admission by the bullied wife of failings and deficiencies that are none too clear to her. These admissions are perfectly sincere, not conscious deceptions. Where there is coercion, conscious deception, the cynical and deliberate decision to give them what they want, does not require explanation. For that matter, a new viewpoint, a new conviction, may not require explanation either; people change their minds. But these are not cases either of cynical submission or of new convictions. They are, again, another form of thinking, another frame of mind, altogether.

In all these cases the individual's objective relation to external reality, including the normal attitude of judgment, is suspended or disabled, at least within the relevant area, and a sense of conviction, a clear subjective sense of what one actually believes, vanishes with it. Sometimes a suspension of critical judgment or "rational thinking" is explicitly demanded by coercive authority. For example, in a widely publicized case of alleged sexual abuse of children, one of the accused, under intense pressure to remember and confess, was instructed to "not try to think about anything" (Wright, 1994).[2] Probably more often, the normal attitude of judgment and, with it, genuine belief in what one says is simply inhibited and in that way disabled in the face of coercion. In any case, it is plain that the various forms of coercive "thought control" or "brainwashing" do not operate in a direct and simple manner. They operate, rather, through a mediating process in which the normal interest in reality and the normal attitude of judgment is lost. Existing ideas cannot be directly expunged from the mind and new ones simply inserted. Such things cannot be accomplished by coercion. But the disabling or inhibition of active judgment of reality apparently can. What one knows, one knows and there is no way to not know. But knowing the answers is not enough if there are ways to prohibit asking oneself the questions.

The evidence is strong that the subjects of coercion never do come to believe, in the ordinary sense, that they did what they did not do. They never sound like their heart is in what they say, never sound like they really mean it. But they can be brought to the point where they are unable to sustain disbelief. To be more exact, they cannot sustain the capacity to make a genuine judgment, to consider the matter, either to believe or disbelieve. The bullied and intimidated wife does not dare even to look at her angry husband. Much less can she bring herself to deliberately and clearly consider what he is saying and, perhaps more to the point, what he is doing. From her standpoint and probably from his as well, merely to regard him that way, to look at him objectively, is an act of brazen defiance. In these circumstances, only acceptance and "agreement"—that is, only an abandonment of the normal act of judgment—can dispel anxiety. It therefore happens that the coerced subject joins the coercive effort. The intimidated wife finally reminds herself of her supposed failings, perhaps even of failings that are not entirely clear to her, often with shame, but never with conviction.

In much the same way, the accused sex offender cited previously finally agreed that he remembered the acts he had initially denied. It was noted by a detective present at the time, however, that the language of his confession was filled with "would've"s and "must have"s. At the conclusion of his confession, the accused man said: "Boy, it's almost like I'm making it up, but I'm not." He was right; he was not deliberately giving them what they wanted. His confession was the result of more complicated processes than a simple deception of his interrogators. He was deceiving himself. Another of the accused, in the same case, also recovered "memories" of acts she had initially been unable to remember. She remarked that this memory was, however, "different" from her "normal memory."

The experience seems to be identical to that reported by Lifton (1963) of subjects of Chinese "thought reform." One such person says: "You begin to believe all this, but it is a special kind of belief . . ." Lifton speaks in this connection of a "surrender of personal autonomy" and describes its mental state as one of "neither sleep nor wakefulness, but rather an in-between hypnogogic state." He notes, also, the peculiar manner of speech of those still influenced by their "reform" experience. He describes his subjects as "speaking only in cliches," "parroting . . . stock phrases," and such. It is clearly not a conversational manner of speech, speech aimed at communication with the listener. It is not speech in which the speaker "means it" or feels genuine conviction for what he says. It is ritualistic speech.

The unconvincing political confessions, the supposed memories recovered under police interrogation or therapeutic insistence and the cliches and "stock phrases" of the subjects of thought reform are in fact radical, externally induced versions of the artificial manner of speech, lacking in conviction and sense of responsibility for what is said, that, as I said earlier, Kaiser recognized in his neurotic patients. This leads us to a further, interesting, conclusion. It seems that the suspension of conviction aimed at relieving the anxiety of coercive threat is in its form not essentially different from what we see activated in neurotic individuals by internally generated anxiety. In other words, coercion and external threat engage the same self-protective reactions of the individual that we find in psychopathology. One might say that the sorts of extreme self-deception that appear in coercive circumstances, the suspension of conviction and the ritualistic speech, constitute a situational psychopathology.

We can identify in common neurotic symptoms and traits the same kinds of self-deception, in this case characterological rather than situational, as in coercive situations. For example, the state of mind characteristic of the hysteric's suggestibility, lacking in deep conviction, seems essentially identical to that in cases of recovered memory or false confession. Or, the tendency of obsessional people to arrive at conclusions that are not without logic, yet utterly unrealistic, on the basis of "must be"s and "might be"s (the tiny red spot on the pizza "might be" blood; it "might" have come from an infected handler) clearly resembles in its form the conscientious effort of the innocent man who, under duress, finally confesses to a crime he did not commit. Here, too, genuine conviction has been suspended. These ideas are not judgments of reality in the ordinary sense, they are not genuine beliefs and they do not sound like it.

I believe that processes of the sort I have just described are evident also in the confessions produced in Soviet-style political show-trials. The anxiety or terror of the situation can be dispelled only by a suspension of judgment and, indeed, of interest in reality and the acceptance of, even conscientious participation in, the accuser's "logic." The resulting confession is, again, a ritual. Artur London, who describes the conditions ("You must trust the party. Let it guide you.") that led to his confession of political crimes in Czechoslovakia in his book, The Confession (1971), says "It was no longer a matter of facts or truth, but merely of formulations, a world of scholastic and religious heresies." London's wife, who eventually accepted her husband's guilt, says, "It was not possible for me to be right and the Party wrong." She did not dare but to suspend judgment and genuine conviction, and with it, of course, an internal sense of responsibility for what she was doing.

Some writers have argued that the capacity for self-deception is, after all, adaptive: man must have his illusions. They are thinking, I assume, of so called "positive illusions," illusory hopes that sometimes, like placebos, contribute to their own fulfillment. I think those benefits of self-deception are small and would not weigh much against its costs. No matter, human anxieties of internal or external origin require its mitigating effect whatever its costs. It is true that there are limits to self-deception in the specific sense that it is never completely successful and completely secure. It does not achieve conviction; genuine belief remains present, only for the time being out of reach. And, in fact, coerced self-deception evidently does dissipate when coercion ceases. The subjects of Chinese thought reform evidently regain their normal judgment after they are released. But the case of self-deception driven by internal anxieties is different. It can be momentary or it can last a lifetime, and no one is qualified to recognize it in himself, much less correct it.

Notes

1 The distinction I am making is essentially the same as the one Fingarette (1969) makes between thoughts that are "spelled out" and those not, and the distinction Bach (1981) makes between "thinking" and "believing" something.
2 I am told that methods of hypnotic trance induction also commonly include the request to avoid critical thinking.

References

Bach, K. (1981) An analysis of self-deception. *Philosophy and Phenomenological Research, 41*(3), 351–370.

Fingarette, H. (1969). *Self-deception*. Berkeley University of California Press.

Kaiser, H. (1955) The problem of responsibility in: psychotherapy. *Psychiatry, 18*, 205–211.

Lifton, R. J. (1963) *Thought reform and the psychology of totalism: a study of "brainwashing" in China*. New York: Norton.

London, A. (1971) *The confession*. New York: Ballantine Books.

Werner, H. (1948) *Comparative psychology of mental development*. Chicago: Follett.

Wright, L. (1994) *Remembering satan*. New York: Knopf.

Chapter 3

Two kinds of conscientiousness

A colleague of mine who was present when I gave a talk on which Chapter 1 is based asked an unsettling question. She asked whether there was no room at all in this psychological view of human behavior for shame and moral accountability[1]. It is not an unfamiliar question, surely not to philosophers nor to lay people. It is raised often in one way or another in discussions of specific moral or legal judgments. The subject is familiar, also, in a specific question regarding psychotherapy. The question is whether a person's understanding of the reasons for his behavior, as is likely to happen in psychotherapy, but not only there, does not nullify moral accountability and weaken moral values by making them irrelevant. The same question may be asked, of course, in connection with the evaluation of others' behavior. The question calls for a closer look at the psychology of moral responsibility or accountability and the shame that is associated with it, and their relation to actual moral values. I shall propose that the relation is not as tight as might be supposed.

Let us assume that what we mean by moral responsibility or accountability is contained in the thought and the experience of imperatives addressed to ourselves: "I should (or shouldn't) have done that." We commonly call that voice in which we address ourselves, mostly silently, but sometimes out loud, the voice of our conscience. But in fact it is only one kind of conscience, reflecting one kind of conscientiousness, that is expressed in this way, and not the only one. If one is interested, it is not hard to discern in most people two markedly different sorts of conscientiousness, although they are not often distinguished in discussion or literature. The kind I just mentioned is notable above all for its self-consciousness. People who are especially conscientious in this way may hover over themselves like an anxious teacher or parent might watch over a child, ready with reminders, not always gentle, of the right kind of attitudes and behavior and the importance of duties and obligations, and ready also to correct, sometimes even punish, personal failings in such matters. That watchful and critical self-awareness constitutes the individual's moral or quasi-moral accounting of his behavior to himself. It may include admonishments by the individual to himself of the sort I mentioned, sometimes mild, sometimes urgent, and in the not uncommon case of transgressions, punishment in the form of self-inflicted shame. The experience is surely familiar to everyone, though much more and more acutely to some than to others.

But there is another kind of conscientiousness that is far less self-conscious and at the same time far more reliable as a determinant of action. This is so because it simply expresses the person's actual values and affections as distinct from those he or others think he should have. His actions according to these values and affections reflect his wishes and convictions rather than a submission, often implicitly grudging, to rules or general precepts. These two kinds of subjective experience can be described as, respectively, a conscientiousness of rules and a conscientiousness of conviction. They are, of course, not mutually exclusive in anyone's makeup, nor even in a particular action, though one or another will predominate. The terms, conscientiousness of rules and conscientiousness of conviction, are to some extent self-explanatory, but let me enlarge on their meaning a little more, as well as on their developmental history.

The morality of the child develops out of his respect for adult authority, both as teacher and model. The child's moral judgments are initially based on a literal acceptance of that authority as absolute. The way things are to be done or not done, the definition of what should be done and what should not, what is good and what is bad—all of these rely heavily on or issue from the adult world. The moral authority of the adult is not the product of coercion; it is simply the source of this kind of judgment. As the child continues to develop, however, the external moral authority and prestige of the adult world is translated by the child into his own rules and regulations. As the psychologist Jean Piaget says, "At a given moment the child thinks that lies are bad in themselves and that, even if they are not punished, one ought not to lie" (p. 194). These rules and regulations retain, subjectively, the quality of quasi-external authoritative imperatives, but are interpreted and applied by the child to particular situations as his own. The moral imperatives of adult authority gradually become internalized and the child achieves some sense of the authority of his own moral judgment. But to the extent that his judgment continues to rely on the authority of the adult, it is a borrowed authority, still not autonomous, not completely the child's own. In effect, it is received dogma (Shapiro, 2000). With further development this emulated or borrowed authority is in turn superseded, and for adolescents, moral judgment and values, though still leaning on the authority of others, including their peers, are asserted, often emphatically, as their own. Eventually, if all goes well, some will become their own. They judge and act, then, according to their own lights, according to values or principles or affections, consciously articulated or not, that they genuinely feel or believe in. This is what I mean by a conscientiousness of conviction, as distinct from the earlier conscientiousness of rules.

We know, however, from everyday observation of others and ourselves, and it is even more clear from clinical observation, that the individual's self-conscious direction of his behavior in emulation of figures of seeming authority and according to authoritative-seeming rules of what should and should not be done, thought or felt does not disappear. In the lives of some people, in fact, consciousness of such admonitory "should"s and "should not"s, sometimes mild, sometimes urgent, plays a central role. In fact, those admonitions addressed by the individual to himself directing what he should or should not do, think or feel, and the sense of accountability that accompanies them, sometimes have the effect of alienating the individual from his actual feelings and wishes and judgments. Indeed, the "shoulds" and "should not"s may be insistent enough to virtually suffocate the individual's actual wishes, feelings, and values. The person loses a clear sense of what those are and imagines that he actually thinks, feels, and wants to do what he only believes he should think, feel, and want to do. The young woman thinks she *wants* to marry her suitor when, actually, she only believes he is the kind of man she *should* marry. It is this attitude of accountability to subjectively authoritative, quasi-moral "should"s and "should not"s that I call a conscientiousness of rules.

These "should"s or "should not"s refer to moral or quasi-moral rules or principles that are not necessarily clearly articulated. They may be only implicit in a continuing attitude of deference to direction whose authority feels superior to and safer than one's own. That attitude of deference to superior authority is expressed subjectively in the sense of obligation or duty to comply. Specific rules or principles may become articulate only when, accompanied by discomfort, they are breached. They may be simple, but widely inclusive, rules of thumb, including conventional admonitions relating to practical matters of everyday living, but still carrying some moral weight (one should finish what one starts, one should not waste, one should not pass up opportunity, etc). It is typically a nagging, burdensome conscientiousness. If it results in further action, it is likely to be action done largely or even entirely for the sake of having done it, to check it off the list, more for personal relief from one's own nagging than out of genuine interest in its supposed objective. The businessman, telling himself that he should finish some work, takes his briefcase home every night, though he never opens it. This kind of obligatory action is likely to be formalistic, like action that is legally required. One should spend every Saturday morning with the children. In the extreme case such action becomes ritualistic; even a semblance of a rational objective is lost and the action is easily identifiable as a symptom. Thus, even though the individual has just washed his hands, he thinks he should wash them again, "just in case," and may settle finally on a precise number of required washings. It is true, though, that the nature of the motivation is not an infallible measure of the value of its result, and the product of even largely ritualistic action may be objectively valuable.

A conscientiousness of rules, or "should"s, carries an authority that feels in some degree outside and above the subject. Inasmuch as it is not autonomous, does not express one's own judgment and values, it does not carry complete conviction. It can be an effective goad to action, but it is never wholehearted. Obligatory action always contains an inner reservation and an implied resistance. It is in the effort to overcome that reservation or resistance that its moral imperatives are very often insistent and often unceasing, and take on the quality of a nagging of the self. That resistance to the demands of this kind of conscience ultimately shows itself in a way that is familiar to everyone; no one actually does all that he thinks he should do, and no one refrains from all that he thinks he should not do. Indeed, no one does all that he thinks he should do even when he has persuaded himself that he really wants to. Thus, we have the ironic result that the kind of conscientiousness that demands moral accountability, the conscientiousness of "should"s, is also the kind that carries the least conviction and is therefore the most likely to be violated. The regular consequence of those failures to do or not do what one should is self-reproach and, often, the punishment of shame.

All this is different for a conscientiousness of conviction. To the extent that action simply follows from values that one genuinely believes in and from genuine affections it does not require or involve this self-conscious, watchful nagging. It does not require a moral accounting and, barring external obstacles, it is not likely to be violated and be the occasion of self-reproach and shame. In that way it is far more effective objectively and far less noticeable subjectively than the conscientiousness of rules. Still, the two attitudes, different as they are, are not mutually exclusive in a person. Both attitudes are surely represented in most, perhaps all, people, though in quite different proportions.

The fact is, however, that people often do not know what their real values are. They are expressed in action, but they are mostly silent. The moral obligations with which they badger themselves and the emulation of figures or constructed images of imagined superiority often leads people to mistaken ideas of their actual moral principles or values. They wish to believe and sometimes come to believe that the values that they think should be theirs actually are theirs. They come to believe, often, that their values are more high minded and less blemished than they actually are or even, realistically, can be. This inevitably has the result of the person's continuing struggles with himself. These struggles are manifest in a vacillation between shame at what he sees as his shortcomings and a self-conscious effort to deny those shortcomings and to live up to an admired image. The following episode, from an exchange in psychotherapy, illustrates such a struggle in a way more explicit than most.

The patient was a European-born professor in his late 50s, who had reluctantly acceded to his wife's urging that he see a therapist. She believed, correctly, that he was severely depressed. This exchange took place 6 or 8 months after the therapy began and after his depression had lifted to some extent, though by no means entirely. On this occasion he entered the therapist's office with his usual dignified and quiet greeting, but seeming even more grave than usual. He sat down and after a short pause, looking directly and, as it seemed, unflinchingly, at the therapist, he began to speak in his careful and rather formal manner. That manner, his facial expression, even his posture conveyed a determination to say what he had to say, however difficult it was.

Patient: The time has come to tell you something that I have never told anyone else; only my wife knows.

He continued:

> You probably have assumed I am Catholic, if you thought about it at all (his surname was a common one in his Catholic country of birth). But actually I am a Jew.

He then very briefly told the story of changing his identity during the war years in Europe. He went on, speaking with difficulty, adding that after the war and his move to America he had "allowed" (though more likely encouraged) the false impression of his identity to continue. His wife had known him during the war and so she knew the truth, but even his children, now adults, did not. He was ashamed, and the longer he had continued the deception, the greater his shame about it and, of course, the more difficult to rectify it. He concluded in an unusual way, quieter and more grave than ever:

> *Patient:* I have always wanted to regard myself as an honorable person, but in this way I have not been that.

The last, however, was said in a voice and with a fleeting glance at the therapist that contained a hint of uncertainty, in addition to its slight qualification ("in this way").

As he continued it became clear that this problem had tormented him for many years. Or, more exactly, he had tormented himself about it episodically over many years. For the most part, during this time, it was more or less out of mind. Often, however, on account of his sensitivity to the issue, mention of some matter even distantly related to its subject caught his attention. This was enough to prompt him to remind himself of his deception and his shame. Once reminded, he silently began what seemed very much like a silent, but agitated, trial. He charged himself with failing to be honorable on account of his deception. This charge would be followed by a less than confident defense, with excuses that were not entirely convincing to him, and reminders to himself of various contrary instances when he had behaved with integrity. The result was invariably inconclusive. He could defend his deception during the war years and the chaotic time afterward, with some success, though even then with a degree of uncertainty. But the fact still remained that he had continued the deception at a time when there was no danger to justify it, in fact only the possibility, which he did not overlook in his report, of some practical advantage in continuing it. In all this, he could not accept a verdict that he was not an honorable man, but neither was he able to acquit himself of the charge he made against himself with conviction. The internal trial went back and forth in this way, with considerable distress, ceasing inconclusively when he was distracted by other matters, and resuming before long.

This man tried to believe that he lived up to a moral standard that, on account of external circumstances and the facts of his own psychology, he had not and could not do. He wanted and tried to believe that he was morally absolutely uncompromising, always rising above the temptations of expediency, his image of an "honorable man," but the facts showed that he was not. The absolute moral standard, which did not allow for human weakness, that he wanted to believe was his standard was in fact not his standard; he was not invariably above choosing the expedient, rather than the principled, course. That standard was only the standard that he thought should be his. It was a standard of behavior, a kind of conscientiousness, that was not an expression of what actually was and what was not acceptable to him under given circumstances, but was derived from quasi-external principles and images that were, probably in other instances as well as this one, unrealistic, perhaps for anyone. It was therefore not remarkable that this standard was not consistently satisfied. A conscientiousness of "should"s, lacking as it is in complete conviction, and containing as it does an element of reservation or resistance, is, as I said, never consistently observed. The result of this failure was continuing shame and his continuing and futile efforts to quiet the shame. It became obvious that the larger part of the reasons for his continued deception was, ironically, shame at the deception itself.

The reduction of this man's shame in psychotherapy did not result in a weakening of his actual moral attitudes or values. It had no effect on those attitudes or values; they were an integral aspect of his personality. But an easing of shame did allow a corresponding relaxation of the effort to sustain an already failing self-deception, that he was what he thought he should be, a person whose values would never permit, however useful or even necessary it seemed at the time, such a deception. He had not, as he had thought, violated his real personal values; those values were in fact much to his credit. He had violated only what he thought should be, and tried to believe actually were, his personal values.

Let me make the point more generally. An individual's empathic understanding of the reasons for behavior he may have thought shameful, and the consequent reduction of that shame, does not undermine or weaken his values. On the contrary, it reveals his actual values and their limitations. It weakens only his self-deception. Thus the person described was a decent, conscientious man before his empathic understanding of the reasons for his behavior, and he remained a decent, conscientious man afterward, only less troubled and with fewer moral pretensions.

Before leaving this subject I want to return briefly to the question raised by my colleague that I mentioned at the beginning of this chapter: she asked whether there was no place for moral accountability and shame in a world that understands and accepts that individuals have reasons that seem to them decisive for doing what they do. Let us say that we recognize that even behavior that is repellent to us must have seemed from its subject's point of view the only next thing to do. Does this recognition invalidate the logic of moral judgment and the basis for shame? It is not hard to imagine what the person who asked that question was thinking. One only has to recall one or another of the despicable crimes reported in the morning paper to realize that a world without shame, in which no one would be accountable and, everyone, whatever they might do and whatever pain they might inflict on others, would be free of shame, is unacceptable.

It is not that we are incapable of understanding the reasons for even the most despicable of crimes. We can, in principle at least and sometimes even in practice, given sufficient information, understand the perpetrator's reasons for doing what he did. In that way, again in principle, we might even be able to empathize with him. *But we do not want to.* We do not want to understand him because his action offends our values and repels us. We want him to be punished. We do not want to empathize with that person for the very reason that it would weaken our wish that he be punished. We want him to feel ashamed.[2] For the same reason we may resist empathic understanding of ourselves. We may feel that we deserve to be punished, to be shamed, not to be understood. Let us remember the psychotherapy patient described in the previous chapter who initially rejected such understanding and the relief from self-reproach and shame that it promised with the angry charge to the therapist, "You're trying to make me feel better!" The two interests, the one of empathic understanding and the other of moral accountability, and their accompanying attitudes are, as we saw in Chapter 1, intolerant of each other, at least in the given moment. What may be our general good will and interest in the empathic understanding of other people can easily be dispelled by actions of theirs that damage, offend, or frustrate our values, affections, or material aims. It follows from this that our inclination either toward empathic understanding of an action or toward moral accountability and shaming will be influenced, perhaps decisively, by the nature of our values, interests, and sensitivities and, as well, our personal relation to the action and its perpetrator. These conditions, for better or worse, place limits not on our general capability, but in any particular instance, on our willingness to understand empathically.

It is interesting to note, incidentally, that this relativity of empathy and moral accountability is recognized in the training of psychotherapists. Psychotherapists are generally able to maintain an empathic interest in patients whose behavior might prompt others, and might otherwise prompt them, to call for shame. This is not because therapists have a loftier outlook or a warmer heart than others, but because they have a special purpose and a special interest in understanding. Even so, that interest has its limits. New therapists are taught to avoid extra-therapeutic relationships of significance, romantic relationships, business relationships, etc., with their patients because those relationships may compete with the therapeutic interest in empathic understanding. No one can be counted on for empathic understanding of their business partner's cheating of them.

Note

1 I am indebted to Professor Arien Mack for raising this question.
2 My reasoning here is similar to that proposed by P. F. Strawson (1962).

References

Piaget, J. (1997) *The moral judgment of the child*. New York: Free Press.
Shapiro, D. (2000) *Dynamics of character*. New York: Basic Books.
Strawson, P. F. (1962) Freedom and resentment. *Proceedings of the British Academy*, 48, 187–211.

Chapter 4

The self-control muddle

There is a problem with the concept of self-control and it appears early, with definitions. The Diagnostic Statistical Manual of Mental Disorders (DSM-5, 2013), in general use in American clinical psychological and psychiatric work, describes a broad category of psychiatric conditions it calls "Impulse-control disorders." A wide range of symptomatic conditions are included in this category such as problem gambling (continued gambling "despite repeated, unsuccessful efforts to stop"), "intermittent explosive disorder," which may include temper tantrums or assaults ("uncontrollable rage" or "failure to resist aggressive impulses"), and kleptomania ("failure to resist impulses"). The alcoholic, similarly, while expressing "a persistent desire . . . and report(ing) multiple unsuccessful efforts to cut down," suffers from "impaired control." A general conception of human action is contained in these diagnostic descriptions. Action in all these cases, it is thought, is the product of "impulses" or, sometimes, "rising tension" or, as others describe it, "urges" the subject fails to control, sometimes despite his "persistent desire." However, a question arises on a matter that is fundamental to all these formulations. Is the desire to stop real? Is there really a wish to resist the impulse, the rising tension or the urge? Or is there, rather, a willingness to allow it? Is the failure to resist actually a failure? These are questions that are by no means necessarily lost even on the proponents of this view. The occasional claim of absolutely irresistible impulse, for example, has met general skepticism. There is no doubt that the gamblers, the drinkers, even the wife beaters typically believe their desire to resist temptation or provocation to be genuine and wholehearted and that their disclaimer of responsibility for the consequent action is generally sincere. But sincere people, as we have seen, sometimes deceive themselves.

Let us begin to answer the question by considering the conception of human action on which these cases are based; that is, action conceived as a product of urges or impulses or tensions that may or may not be controllable. This is a common enough picture of action, derived from behaviorist psychology although it is not absent in psychoanalytic theory as well. But it is a simplistic picture of human action, one that might describe the action of a trained animal, not that of a person. Human action, any human action, is much more complicated than that. In humans, certainly in adult humans, urges or impulses can account, as I said; only for temptations; they cannot in themselves account for action.

As we have seen in the Introduction, the quality or form of action develops, along with cognitive development, becoming increasingly reflective and deliberate from infancy through adolescence. As the objective quality of action develops, so does its subjective experience. In general, the more deliberate and planned the action is, the greater the consciousness of its choice and of responsibility for what is said and done. These developmental features, increased reflectiveness, self-awareness, and deliberateness, are constituents of the normal sense responsibility for what one says and does. Of course, not all action, probably not most of it, is fully deliberate. Much action is spontaneously reactive or simply habitual and more or less unselfconscious. But it is spontaneous or habitual only within deliberate limits. One usually becomes conscious of those limits and of one's own behavior when the limits are approached. The spontaneous joke at a friend's absent-minded mistake is cut short with a sense of going too far at a small sign of his sensitivity, or even at no sign from him at all. No spontaneous action, no impulse or urge comes into existence except in a context of mind, of aims, attitudes, and imaginative possibilities. That context is both a source and a filter of action. There is no way for people to circumvent this context of mind in doing what they do, however much they may be tempted or provoked by what is around them. The simple fact is that humans are thinking, imaginative creatures who, when they act, are aware, to one degree or another, of doing so, and are very much and, as a rule, very flexibly in charge of what they do or say, whether they notice it or not.

It is true that the nature and range of spontaneous or habitual action, the range of what is automatically allowable in given circumstances and what is not, is different in different sorts of personality. Some people are given to spur-of-the-moment action—these are the people who are usually called impulsive—and others are generally more reflective and deliberate. For those impulsive people, to whom decision and action come swiftly and easily, with comparatively little reflection, the consciousness of responsibility for what is done or said is accordingly fainter. It is easier for those people to feel little or no responsibility even for consequential action. They will be able to say, "I couldn't help it," or "I didn't mean to do it" without conflict. But it is just the point that even those impulsive individuals—in the extreme example, psychopaths or sociopaths—though they may lack, or avoid, long-range interests and high moral values and principles, are still not without some persistent aims and relevant attitudes of their own, aims and attitudes that provide or impose an imaginative context for any action. If, speaking of sociopaths, their actions do not arise from idealistic attitudes, they are reflections of cynical and opportunistic ones. If they are lacking in long-range plans, they are mindful of immediate arrangements. But whether it is an idealistic scientist or a cynical holdup man, there is no human action that is not the product of an active and complicated mind, a person in some degree conscious of himself and what he is doing as he forms intentions and makes choices. In short, all human action is to one degree or another imaginative and volitional. It is never a matter simply of the discharge of urges or the execution of impulses.

The simplistic conception of personal action shows its shortcomings also in its conception of restraint. For if personal action is conceived as simply driven by impulses and urges, it is necessary to posit some sort of psychological faculty that is superior to and therefore capable of resisting or transcending those impulses and urges. This conception already hints at a kind of self-transcendence that becomes more explicit in the concept of willpower discussed in the following chapter. In fact, some such faculty has been posited and thought to be the source of the conscious effort of restraint or the ability to delay satisfaction. It has been compared to a muscle that may be strong or weak (Baumeister & Heatherton 1996; Baumeister Vohs & Tice, 2007). As one considers the logic of this conception of self-control, one might easily have the sensation of traveling in a circle. This understanding tells us little more than what is necessary for self-control is having a strong self-control muscle. It does not tell us what this muscle is or what its strength consists of or how it works. Indeed, it cannot tell us much more about restraint because its conception of action has omitted the volitional processes that account for both the nature of action and the nature of restraint.

Self-control or the capacity for restraint is no more than an aspect of those volitional processes. To say that action is the product not of urges, but of a complicated imaginative process, a process involving a context of relevant attitudes, of prior aims and interests, finally of choices, is to speak not just of the nature of action but of the nature of restraint of action or self-control, as well. For restraint of action, self-control is another volitional action, another product of an imaginative mind, another choice. The question has been asked (Baumeister & Heatherton 1996), for example, how to account for the self-control, the restraint, of nonviolent civil rights activists when they are brutally attacked. How can they restrain the natural urge or impulse to strike back? The answer that they must have sufficient strength of self-control takes us, as I said, in a circle. The answer, rather, lies in all the factors of personal makeup, present circumstances and, especially, the immediate aims that give rise to the individual's choice of action, including the action that we commonly call restraint of action or self-control. Thus we can say of civil rights activists, who have been taught the principles of nonviolence, that their impressive restraint, even when they are brutalized, consists precisely of their deep belief in and commitment to nonviolence. The "strength" of their self-control, the extent of their resistance to provocation, can be measured by the depth of that value. It consists of the existence of that value. It is the same value system that in various forms orders much of the rest of their action.

It is much the same in every case: how is the student who has an exam the next day able to turn down an invitation to a movie? What gives her the strength? The answer is she is in general a conscientious person who believes in trying to do her best, or perhaps she is also an ambitious person who wants a good grade or, possibly, she wants to hold on to her scholarship. What gives the young doctor the strength to continue at work when he is so tired? The answer is, again, that he believes that it is a doctor's duty to look after his patients, or, by no means a minor consideration, he wants to complete his residency. Values and aims like those are determinants of what people decide to do and what they decide not to do, and they are the source of their "strength." Any mindful action, and there is no other kind, includes both a purpose and restraint of contrary action that would interfere with that purpose.

This is not to say, of course, that restraint is always subjectively easy or, without internal conflict or regret, or that it does not sometimes involve an individual's intense or prolonged struggles with himself. Aims and values, distant and immediate, are likely to compete in many choices. When restraint is achieved after such acute or prolonged conflict it may include a sense of special effort, and may easily be understood by its subject as achieved only by recourse to a special faculty or "muscle" or a kind of self-transcendence, a sacrifice of the stronger or more immediate desire for the lesser, but morally superior or more distant one. But in fact moral values and imperatives or more distant aims or, for that matter, ordinary caution or conventional propriety, may simply outweigh and diminish in perspective, not necessarily without some regret, the immediate temptation. This does not require a special faculty of control or self-transcendence; it is only the subjective aspect, sometimes complicated and not smooth, of ordinary volitional action.

It is worth noting that a related problem has been present in psychoanalysis. Its older theory of early cognitive development and, also, its general conception of defense mechanisms contain dubious and unnecessary conceptions of restraint. Thus an elementary capacity for restraint or delay of satisfaction was thought by Freud and later psychoanalytic theoreticians to provide a structural basis for cognitive development. But the psychological process that constituted such a capacity for delay of satisfaction was never clear. A more plausible conception would see that relationship in the opposite direction, that is, the capacity for delay as a result rather than a prerequisite of cognitive development. The teacher who engages his or her students in an interesting project will have an orderly class. Similarly, the idea of the defense mechanisms as impulse controlling or restraining agencies are better replaced by the concept of styles of activity that, like any organizing function, are restrictive or limiting in some directions even while expressive in others.

If it can be said of self-control that it is no more than a subjective aspect of normal volitional action, can the same understanding be applied to the supposed failure or inability to maintain self-control? In other words, can it be said that the case of apparent failure of self-control is, again, no more than a kind, in some cases even a characteristic style, of volitional action? The clearest cases of impulsive or reckless, sometimes even criminal, action that may easily be considered emblematic of such failure are the individuals we call psychopaths or sociopaths. These are people who are, as I have said, generally without a strong presence of stable, long-range aims and deep values or principles. Accordingly, they are very reactive to immediate circumstances, whether opportunities or provocations. On account of that they are likely to lead quite erratic lives, changing jobs, locations, relationships easily and often. From their standpoint an opportunity is not just an opportunity-to-be-considered. The immediacy of their reactions, the absence of reservations, gives it the quality of an actual enticement or a simple trigger of action. Thus, the thief says, "the money was just laying there." Claims of that kind may be no more than efforts to minimize culpability, of course; they may even be extended to a defensive claim that the attraction (or the provocation) was absolutely irresistible. Even so, there is a certain basis in these individuals' attenuated experience of decision and action for their disclaimer of personal responsibility and assignment of responsibility to its external trigger. It is a style of volitional action that is, as I said, characteristic of individuals of a certain sort of personality. It hardly seems reasonable to describe such action as a failure or loss of self-control since there is little or no interest in restraint in the first place.

More moderate examples of comparative lack of restraint are those mildly impetuous people, most often though by no means exclusively women, who are also described as flighty or frivolous. The description may easily be condescending, but it does seem to capture a particular feminine identity that, while out of date, is not totally extinct (Lakoff 1977). These people do not take themselves entirely seriously. They sometimes say, sincerely and without embarrassment, that they are guided in life by their emotions. In other words, they do not regard their action as fully intended by them, do not feel fully responsible for it. For example, one woman, changing her mind after she had impetuously left her husband for a romantic adventure, pleaded that she had been "just kidding." In these cases, too, the absence of restraint of impulsive acts is actually an absence of serious interest in restraint. It is, again, an aspect of a style of volitional action, hardly a failure of self-control.

Despite the common acceptance at face value of supposed inability to restrain impulses to act, the extreme case of absolute irresistibility of urges or impulse whatever the costs or risks has, as I said, met with general doubt and skepticism. It is too hard to believe that the impulse will not be resisted in the face, say, of grave and certain danger. But the nature of this doubt about the reality of the extreme case points to the weakness in the general conception of failure of self-control. The suspicion that a claim of absolute inability to resist impulse hides a willingness to succumb to it may be justified in the general case as well. The clinical evidence confirms that this is so. Let me give a related, highly condensed, example from psychotherapy.

A single man in his mid thirties, employed in the successful family business, came for psychotherapy at the insistence of his socially prominent family. He behaved and spoke with a somewhat exaggerated propriety, producing an effect of a sight stuffiness. He said emphatically that he shared his family's view that something must be done about his excessive drinking. It was clear from his story that despite his semblance of propriety, he was, in his own eyes as well as his family's, the problem and the disgrace of the family, and that they are angry with him. All those involved, both he and his family, agreed that his drinking is "out of control." He insisted, with an evident desire to be believed, that he wanted desperately to stop his binges, adding for emphasis, that when he drinks he sometimes does "terrible things." He said this sounding like a scolded child who knows he has been bad. However, he continued, with what seemed a somewhat forced regret, to say "but I'm a weak person." One could not avoid the thought at that point that this image of himself as "weak" was important in an effort to exculpate him from full responsibility for his action. Nevertheless, he seemed quite sincere in his own belief that he meant what he said.

Here is a condensed excerpt from an early psychotherapy session.

Patient: I know I have a problem with drinking and I'll do anything you ask to overcome it. Anything! That's what I'm here for!

He proceeded, with the same disapproval, to outline the nature of the problem. He does not drink continuously, apparently, but he has frequent binges.

Patient: When I go to a party and people are drinking I can't refuse. I'm a weak person, I admit it. So I have one or two drinks thinking that won't be a problem. But then, after two drinks, I'm gone . . . and (looking somewhat exaggeratedly remorseful) I end up doing terrible things!
Therapist: Maybe you have an example in mind.
Patient: (reluctantly, disapprovingly) . . . Well, the last one, the one that is responsible for my being here was at my cousin's wedding. . . . I got drunk and acted very . . . well. . . . I finally got up on a table and sang. My cousin and my parents were very upset. They were furious.

But as he continued to describe the event a flicker of a smile crosses his face. In fact, he seems to be making an effort to suppress laughter.

Therapist: You seem to be trying not to laugh.
Patient: No, no, there was a big commotion. There was nothing funny about it.
Therapist: Judging by your expression, I'm not so sure.
Patient: Well . . . (again a disapproving look, but then, emitting short, bark-like laughs that he struggles to suppress) . . . Well, I guess it was funny in a way.
Therapist: In a way?

After further, fruitless, effort to suppress his amusement, he described the event. With a kind of strangled glee, still mixed with disapproval, he described the consternation his behavior evoked from the family and others present. Shortly, he proceeded to talk about his drinking in a different way, with a genuineness that had not appeared before. He made a striking observation about himself:

Patient: The thing is, I know I'm a stuffy person. . . . The only time I really feel like myself is when I'm drinking.

It was clear that this man was sincere, though self-deceiving. He believed, or tried to believe, that he was unable to stop his binges despite a wholehearted desire to do so, and that he wanted to reform. He thought that he meant what he said when he expressed a determination to stop drinking. But in actual fact he did not quite mean it. Who could blame him? Who would give up the only thing that made him "feel like myself?" The faintness of his conviction was already unwittingly implied in his early "admission" of weakness. Indeed, that his supposed inability to restrain himself was in fact willingness, or more than willingness, to abandon restraint was suggested then. One might easily imagine that his family, in their angry disapproval, suspected something of the sort all along.

The nature of the therapeutic change indicated in this episode may also be noted. What was originally, from this man's standpoint, a "terrible" failure of self-control due to his "weak character," was experienced by him later as an active choice. Recognition of its purpose, to "feel like myself," even shows it to be a reasoned choice, if one can speak of purpose that is less than consciously articulate in this way. His sense of responsibility for his action, no more than faint at the beginning of this exchange, was clear at its end. It can be said of this person that the volitional level of his drinking rose. That is, his sense of having made a choice (and therefore the possibility of making a different choice) became greater.

Perhaps the example I have just given supports my argument unfairly. The example was of a person whose disapproval of, and sense of responsibility for, his drinking was faint to begin with ("I go to a party and I can't refuse"). Perhaps this makes it too easy to show that his apparent inability for restraint ("after two drinks I'm gone") was actually a willingness to abandon restraint, half-hidden to him by a thin self-deception. It might be objected, in other words, that the faintness of this man's sense of his own intentions and therefore of his disapproval makes it too easy to show an apparent failure of self-control as no more than a style of volitional action. It could reasonably be argued that genuine failure of self-control will show itself more convincingly in the actions of more reflective or determinedly restrained people, where there is a more serious claim by a person of acting against their will, doing something that they definitely did not want to do, but could not resist.

Consider the following case of such a person whose supposed failure of self-control came, although regularly, only after intense, heartfelt struggles with herself. A retired professional woman in her late sixties, quite dignified and, as it turned out, very prideful, who looked quite depressed when she first came to the therapist's office. She was careful to make an unusual point about her reason for coming. She said that she had not come for therapeutic help, but simply to have someone to talk to, after the death of her partner of many years. She said this quietly and evenly. Judging by her comments a number of younger people had been devoted to her and her partner and had turned to them over the years for advice and other kinds of help, but, she explained, because they are all much younger she cannot talk to them in a personal way. She said that she should be available to them, not the other way round. She did not, for several weeks, mention any drinking problem. When she finally did, she spoke of it with obvious shame and difficulty and with a quiet, but fierce, contempt for herself. Her drinking, "only sherry," was episodic, but had become more frequent. She drank until she lost consciousness, repeating this for several days during which she does not go out or answer her phone or any knock on the door.

Here is a condensed report of a single therapy session.

Patient: (after an initial silence, looking ashamed and angry with herself) ... Well, I drank too much again last night.

It is worth noting that this locution, whose form is so common ("I ate too much," "I talked too much," etc.) often itself constitutes a partial disclaimer of responsibility inasmuch as it implies that the action was continued beyond what was wanted or intended. It was that thought that led the therapist to respond as he did:

Therapist: It's more likely, I imagine, that you drank just enough.
Patient: No! I don't want to drink! ... (then, with a different emphasis) I don't want to drink! Obviously something inside me does want to, but *I* don't want to!
Therapist: You sound contemptuous of this "something inside" of you.
Patient: I am contemptuous. I'm failing my responsibility to my friends (the younger people). ... They try to reach me and I don't answer the phone or the door ...
Therapist: Sometimes a person may not feel up to such responsibilities.

She was silent for a while. Then, sounding bitter, but more genuine, less lofty:

Patient: They're not really my friends. They were her (her partner's) friends. They don't give a damn about me. ... Nor I about them.

She talked quietly then for the first time about her partner, their close relationship, how she misses her.

Patient: ... But it's been 6 months, I should be over it.
Therapist: According to what?
Patient: (pauses) ... The doctor tells me I'd better stop drinking (She refers to her serious heart condition, about which the doctor has warned her.). But I don't really care, I just want to forget.

She continues, then, to speak of her grief at the loss of her partner and the relief of alcoholic oblivion.

When this woman's claim that she did not want to drink was abandoned, it was replaced by a recognition not only of her desire to drink, but, also, of its purpose, to forget her grief. Thus when she was able to express herself in this less lofty way, her own picture of her drinking changed significantly. What had seemed, certainly to her, a shameful failure of self-control could then be seen not only as a willingness, but a purposeful determination to do what she had been doing, even at risk to her health.

In my final example the issue of self-control and the claim of an inability for restraint is itself presented not only explicitly, but with unusual emphasis. But this emphatic claim, as we will see, is no measure of its reality. The patient was a young man who had not been married long. In this session he began, immediately upon entering the therapist's office, beseeching him for help with self-control, rather loudly and, it seemed, somewhat theatrically, as though he were making a speech. As if to underscore the urgency of his need, he stood, rather than taking his seat, and paced back and forth.

> *Patient:* Doc, you've got to help me! If I continue like this, it will ruin my marriage!

He then described how he "lost it":

> *Patient:* . . . Last night was really terrible! . . . I threw things around the room, threw a lamp against the wall. . . . It really frightened her (his wife). She was cowering in the corner. . . . It will ruin my marriage! . . .

As he told the story, he seemed to avoid looking at me. I mentioned that to him. He looked surprised, became silent for a moment, then brushed the observation aside as though it were an irrelevant and peculiar interest of mine. It was plain then that he turned away when he could not suppress an incipient smile. It was not an amused smile but, rather, a smile of satisfaction. I told him what I had seen.

> *Therapist:* You seem to try not to smile.

He protested again, but then he ceased his pacing and theatrical manner and, in a more conversational tone, talked about his behavior the previous evening.

Patient: . . . It sure intimidated her.

He explained what provoked his behavior. His wife asked him, late in the evening, to go to the store for a loaf of bread.

Patient: . . . Actually, I don't mind going out like that. But she's bossy and I don't want to be a wimp! I want to be like that character Jack Nicholson played in "One Flew Over the Cuckoo's Nest," you know, a tiger.

I want to emphasize that this man's theatrical performance at home and, later, in my office was not an effort to deceive me. He believed his "terrible" behavior at home and his agitation in my office was genuine. But in fact it was an expression of his wish and his attempt to be a "tiger"; not a "wimp." His pride, when he described his violent and supposedly explosive behavior and its effect on his wife, was barely hidden ("It sure intimidated her"). His behavior had been a performance, in some measure for his wife, but primarily for himself.

Even action that seems self-destructive in its result need not be considered a failure of self-control. In that case, too, before one can speak of a failure of restraint, one must presume a genuine desire for restraint. Of course, there are gamblers who lose, criminals who get caught, addicts and drinkers who ruin their lives. It is true, also, in many of those instances, that a distant cost or penalty is the price of an immediate satisfaction or relief. The drinker or addict endangers his job, the smoker courts serious illness. But it is a mistake to imagine, when we talk of so-called self-destructive action, that short-term satisfactions and long-term consequences are always calculated. They are not. In fact, just such calculations are often avoided: a few drinks, an action so quick that it hardly feels like a decision, a rationalization that emphasizes the single, relatively safe instance of a general risky pattern—all these diminish one's sensation of making a risky choice or any choice at all. That is, they weaken the experience of responsibility for the action and make it easier to claim to oneself, "I can't help it." They are ways in which people, some people especially, but all of us sometimes, can avoid asking ourselves questions to which, we dimly suspect, the answers will be unwelcome.

There is one further consideration that deserves attention here. The idea of an independent faculty of self-control, a muscle with its own strength, hinting at a capacity for self-transcendence, is not secure as a strictly psychological concept. As it is used, it is imbued with moral meaning. What we call self-control invariably refers to avoiding doing something bad or to doing what one should do; failure of self-control means doing something bad or doing what one shouldn't do. Failure to restrain, or giving in to, "urges" or "impulses," is far more likely to mean doing something bad than something good. On the other hand, regarding what we call self-control or a seeming loss of self-control simply as varieties of volitional action strips these concepts of their moral quality. When we regard behavior in that way and survey the wider picture of the variety of styles and subjective experience of human action it is difficult to avoid a conclusion that perhaps common sense as well as logic should have led us to in the first place: what people do is what at the time they want to do. Sometimes they do it for pleasure, sometimes for relief, sometimes for safety, but when they disapprove of, or are otherwise uneasy with, what they are doing, they sometimes do it in ways that allow them to believe that they really didn't mean to do it at all.

References

Baumeister, R. F., & Heatherton, T. F. (1996) Self-regulation failure. *Psychological Inquiry*, 76–79.

Baumeister, R. F., Vohs, K. D., & Tice, D. M. (2007) The strength model of self-control. *Current Directions in Psychological Science*, *16*(6), 351–355.

Diagnostic Statistical Manual of Psychiatric Disorders, Fifth Edition, American Psychiatric Association 2013.

Lakoff, R. (1977) Women's language. *Language and Style*, X(4).

Chapter 5

Will, willpower, free will

The colloquial meaning of will, knowing what one wants to do and taking action to do it, has, I think, its most vivid and clarifying use in a certain negative example. It is the description by the psychiatrist Kurt Goldstein (1941) of the brain-injured patients he studied as "will-less." They were able to complete a cognitive task such as reciting a series of numbers if the series was begun by the examiner, but were unable to begin it themselves. It is an exceptional case, of course, which is why it is useful in distinguishing the desire or wish to accomplish something from a kind of activeness that seems necessary to initiate it.

The concept of will has not been popular with psychologists and psychoanalysts with a few exceptions. It has always sounded too vitalistic and mysterious. It has, however, had an important place in the thinking of those few psychoanalysts, in particular Rollo May (1966), Leslie Farber (1966), and Allen Wheelis (1956). They have turned, or returned, to the concept of will in an effort to remedy the old psychoanalytic problem of which we have already spoken and which will turn up again and again in this book. That is, these analysts have used the idea of will to articulate and emphasize the person's consciously motivated and self-directed activity, in argument against the absence of such activeness and self-direction in psychoanalytic theory and therapy, and that has seemed to them, and to others, to be encouraged by aspects of the psychoanalytic experience. In particular, the assumption of unexceptionable psychological determinism, including especially the decisive influence of unconscious motives that is central to psychoanalytic work, has been thought by them to contradict and undermine the reality and effectiveness of conscious choice or decision, and in doing so has tended to discourage initiative in their patients. It is true, of course, that the fact of psychological determinism is sometimes used to rationalize a disavowal of responsibility for action. Thus

Allen Wheelis (1956), frustrated at the failure of insight alone into childhood family dynamics to produce behavioral change, and dismayed by its apparent encouragement of a passive attitude advocates calling on the patient's will for help. Rollo May, like Leslie Farber, much influenced by the European existentialists, is, similarly, uncomfortable with the psychoanalytic assumption of determinism. He suggests, in objecting to unexceptionable determinism, that consciousness introduces "unpredictable elements" into decision and action, as Wheelis also does, but, even so, he rejects the idea that freedom is only "what is left over" from determinism. May takes pains, however, to present a picture of will that is separate and different from the moralistic and suppressive will of Victorian willpower and to offer a more sympathetic will that is more or less continuous with intention.

Altogether, the resort to the concept of will by these thoughtful writers is an explicitly remedial effort to restore a conception of conscious self-direction to a place in their psychoanalytic work. But its success is doubtful and at times the effort seems less than confident. They have identified a theoretical and therapeutic problem, a conceptual gap, that may in their judgment encourage a certain indecisiveness or inactivity in their analytic patients. But when they assign responsibility for this inaction to a failure or insufficiency of will, they see only a lapse where there must actually be a contrary motivation. And where there is a contrary motivation, the responsibility for the action, or inaction, that follows from it must be laid not at a deficient faculty of will, but a person with reasons of his own. We shall return to this important issue of the relation of psychological determinism to the reality of conscious self-direction and choice shortly. We shall see that the problem arises again in the absence of an adequate conception of volitional action, and that when that absence is rectified the apparent conflict between a deterministic view and the effectiveness of conscious choice disappears, and with it the necessity to call on or invent a special and independent motivational faculty.

In the use of the concept of will in the idea of willpower its status as an independent mental faculty capable of self-transcendence is of course stronger and more explicit. In the conception of at least one version of free will the supposed capacity for self-mastery is still greater. By an exercise of willpower, it is supposed, one can overcome not only obstacles to achieving a desired goal but, more important, discouragement or temptation. In general, willpower is said to enable one to overcome the immediate, but less worthy, temptations in favor of more distant and worthier aims; that is, make oneself do what one should do and overcome the temptation to do what one shouldn't do. In other words, in its customary aims as well as its connotation of self-transcendence, the idea of willpower, like self-control, is not so much a psychological concept, as a moral one. Here, in a stronger version, responsibility for action or inaction is assigned not to the person, but to the strength or weakness of will. It is invoked in the effort against what is seen, from a moral standpoint, as weakness, discouragement, the easy way out. And here, too, the picture of what is seen as weakness, calling for willpower, is from a psychological standpoint the contrary motivation of a person who has reasons for his choice, whether the happiest choice or the least bad choice, though he himself may not know those reasons.

Of course people resist temptations and sacrifice immediate pleasures for more distant aims. They overcome even daunting obstacles and persist in their efforts to achieve a goal, and they often do these things only after struggles with themselves. But a psychological understanding, rather than a moral one, requires a reversal of the order of events. The moralist says: willpower, if it is strong enough, will make it possible for the individual to overcome immediate temptation in favor of more distant aims. The psychologist says, on the contrary, the existence of larger aims (among which may be the avoidance of shame), will place the immediate temptation in perspective. The will to resist immediate temptations or overcome obstacles in pursuit of difficult goals consists of nothing more than the importance of those goals. Where there is a paucity of such long-range goals or permanent values or where such goals seem out of reach, as in the demoralized person or the cynical one, resistance to the immediate satisfaction is accordingly reduced and willpower shows itself as an empty concept.

As is well known, the principle of free will has more than one meaning. In its stronger meaning it postulates the capacity of a person to make choices and take actions that are independent of prior psychological causes. It thus asserts, even more sharply than the concept of willpower, the capacity of the individual to transcend his normal limitations, to act in a way contrary to, and presumably morally superior to, the action to which regular psychological causes or his own psychology might dispose him. Many people think that such capacities are a necessary condition for moral accountability. They reason that a transgressor can be held accountable for his action only if he could have made a different choice as, they assert, he could have done. We shall return in a moment to this critical question of whether an individual could have done something other than what he did.

But free will is commonly understood to have another meaning in which it simply refers to the reality of choice or the act of decision. It takes us to the old and well-worn problem, whether in a world presumed to be strictly determined by a chain of prior causes and their effects, personal choice can be considered free and the effective determinant of action. One thing is clear: no logical or psychological argument can shake the human experience of the reality and effectiveness of personal choice, nor the conviction based on that experience that this choice was not fixed or determined prior to the making of it. But to the person who believes in scientific law it is no less clear that every action, every choice or decision, can be understood and in principle predicted according to unexceptionable principles of cause and effect. If this means that every action is determined by a chain of causes and effects prior to the experience of choice, the effectiveness of choice is no more than an illusion, something like the queen's speech to parliament, since it merely follows an already determined course. This has, indeed, been one psychoanalytic position (Knight, 1954), excepting only that in this case the queen would have convinced herself that she really was directing affairs. The problem is not only a philosophical, or logical, one. It is also a psychological problem. It is even, as we saw in Chapter 1, a problem for psychotherapists. We shall see whether a close examination of the actual formation of a choice can contribute some clarification of it.

It happens, as I have said, that the issue shows itself in an especially sharp form in the process of psychotherapy. Let me say a few words here about that process. It is and must be a fundamental assumption by psychotherapists that all behavior is determined by prior psychological causes and that it can be understood in that way. One may even say that such an understanding of the psychological causes of behavior and the personal reasons in which those causes are expressed will make it clear that any given behavior was inevitable. Thus, psychotherapists assume that even the strangest symptoms can be understood to have their reasons, that these reasons are products of the individual's psychological makeup, products of the way that person sees things and thinks about them in the situation at hand. This understanding is not just of theoretical interest to the psychotherapist; it is basic to the therapeutic work. An essential part of that work consists of the patient's discovery, with the help of the therapist, of these causes and reasons for what he does. He discovers the point of view according to which what he did seemed at the time and in those circumstances the only next thing to do. He discovers a way of seeing things and thinking about them which, while it is his own, he was not at the time clearly aware of. In the course of this discovery, though neither he nor the therapist is likely to take special notice of it as such, the patient is gradually introduced to a deterministic point of view. It is a view of his behavior that is often different from his more familiar, frequently prejudiced, view. Out of this new awareness, actions that may have seemed to the person himself strange, wrong, adventitious, or even unwilling, perhaps actions that were hardly more than ritualistic, actions for which he felt little or no responsibility, come to be understood as having seemed the thing to do, sometimes happily, sometimes only least bad, not perhaps for everyone, but for him, probably not all the time, but at that time.

But that is not the only, nor the most important, result of this process, if it is successful. To discover these actions as having causes, even as having been in principle predictable, on account of this person's makeup and point of view, is to discover his reasons for choosing them. It is to discover that they were not only in principle predictable, but that they were purposeful. For a person to become aware of all this, to become aware of the makeup that gives him reasons for doing just what he does and nothing else is to become aware that he has made, and makes, choices. For him to feel the inevitability, given the way he sees things, of those reasons and that action is to feel the standpoint from which they made sense. It is, therefore, to feel the beginnings of ownership of actions for which he had previously, however much he may have rationalized them, felt little or no responsibility. He is, in other words, introduced at the same time to having made choices and to the fact that making those particular choices and no others was determined by a point of view, by aims and interests that are his. One might even say that those choices were expressions of what he is, though that, of course, is not of his choosing. In short, for a person to be made aware of the causes for how he sees things and the reasons for doing what he does is to be made aware that he has made choices and that, in turn, opens the possibility of his making new choices. We arrive therefore at a conclusion that may seem paradoxical: the empathic, that is, deterministic, understanding of an individual's past action, far from contradicting the subjective experience and the actuality of choice, gives rise to it. Consider the following much condensed account of such an occasion during a particular hour in psychotherapy.

The patient was a 52-year-old divorced man, a scientist, driven and obsessive both in his professional ambition and his pursuit of sexual escapades with women. He and his therapist had talked about the nature of his drivenness many times, especially in connection with his work and his ambition. Like many obsessive people he regularly pressed and nagged himself with the idea that he should do still more of whatever he was doing, should not pass up any opportunity or possibility of gain, should keep trying however small the promise of success, even, in fact, when he did not really believe that there was any possibility of success at all or that the "opportunity" was one that he would actually enjoy. Many times he was able to persuade himself, though with less than complete conviction, that he actually wanted to do what in fact he only felt he should do. On those occasions, however, it was not difficult to perceive in his voice, louder and more emphatic than usual, and the faintly questioning expression of his eyes an absence of genuine enthusiasm. The psychotherapy hour condensed here happened to be at the end of a day in which he had attended a scientific conference. As is common at such conferences, several meetings at which specialized papers are presented were held in different rooms at the same time. He began the hour ruefully describing how he had rushed from one such meeting to another, making frequent stops, also, at the hotel lounge, always out of the same concern:

Patient: You know me, always afraid I might be missing something (in a presentation) or not meeting somebody (who might conceivably advance his career).

It had, in fact, often become apparent both to him and the therapist, that he had very little conviction that these "opportunities" promised any gain. He continued these half-serious reproaches of himself for some time. At a later point in the hour, however, he rather abruptly brightened up:

Patient: Enough! (then, in the manner of making an announcement) I'm going to change the subject . . .

As it turned out, though he did not realize it, he hardly did change the subject. He proceeded to tell about meeting a woman in the hotel lobby that day. He described her ("sexy"). He had gotten her phone number and address and had promised to drop by her place that evening.

Patient: (trying to sound excited) I think she might be available.

He listed her attractions, but in doing so he sounded and looked like a salesman selling a product in which he lacked confidence, and trying to make up for that with a forced enthusiasm.

Therapist: You seem to be trying to work up enthusiasm.

He seemed taken aback but, after a moment, he spoke more quietly and hesitantly.

Patient: Well, it's raining outside ... (pauses) ... and she lives way across town. ... and it probably isn't a sure thing.
Therapist: If you don't feel like it, why bother?

He seemed to search for an explanation.

Patient: (doubtfully, as if wrestling with himself) ... If I don't follow up, that might be the end of it ... She'll lose interest. ... No, I should go.
Therapist: You say you *should* go.
Patient: It's a chance that might not come again.
Therapist: That's the principle?
Patient: (quietly). ... Maybe.

Shortly, the patient leaves. The therapist learns in the following session that he did not go.

Let me review what happened here. This man discovered that the reasons for his initial plan were not entirely as he had imagined them. His plan was not prompted, as he had believed, or tried to believe, simply by libidinal desire. That interest had already been discouraged by the circumstances ("It's raining outside ... she lives way across town") and required some salesmanship to himself to be sustained. His motivation, it turned out, was actually quite different; it was compliance with a vaguely moral, self-imposed imperative (an opportunity should not be wasted; I should go), which initially was not clearly articulated. As that imperative, now emphatically extended ("might not come again"), was consciously articulated, its form was inevitably changed. The recollection of what had been a more or less reflexive reaction according to a vague imperative, triggered by the appearance of an "opportunity," was transformed by its conscious articulation into an experience of a deliberate action, that is, a choice. But the experience of a choice opens the possibility of making a different choice, and that is what he did. Let us make a further surmise regarding the subjective experience that accompanied this change. To the extent that his original plan was in deference to a vaguely sensed imperative, it was plainly not wholehearted. As the effort to sell the idea to himself makes clear, it was not experienced as simply an expression of his spontaneous wish. On the other hand, if, as it seems, his final action was experienced as a conscious and deliberate choice, it must necessarily have felt more completely his own.

When the conception of psychological determinism is considered it is often presented as the determination of action by the chain of cause and effect prior to decision. The idea of the person therefore becomes one of a mere transmitter of prior causes; it is a picture in which the individual's act of decision or choice is clearly superfluous as far as his action is concerned. Decision or choice appears, from this standpoint, as no more than subjectively congruent with, or at most instrumental to, aims that have already been determined. This, as I mentioned, has been the view of conscious choice presented by Robert P. Knight (1954). It may also be this view that has prompted the concern among some thoughtful psychoanalysts that the deterministic conception may encourage an attitude of passivity on the part of their patients. At any rate, that conception of psychological determinism is a misunderstanding, as is shown in the psychotherapy case outlined earlier. In that case the deterministic understanding implied by the individual's recognition of the causes of and reasons for his original plan did not devalue choice. To the contrary, the recognition of the determinants of his plan was not a recognition of the causes of his behavior, but of the causes of his choices, the causes of the reasons for his behavior. The deterministic understanding made him aware that he had reasons for what he did or planned to do, that he did in fact make choices and therefore could make them again, now more consciously and, in this sense, more freely. The result was not passivity, but an increased consciousness of the possibilities of autonomous action. The contradiction between psychological determinism and the reality of effective choice dissolves with the recognition that the causal chain does not end prior to the reasoned and imaginative act of choice, but with that act. The present thinking person, not what caused this person to be what he is and to have the reasons that he has, is the final link in the causal chain. He is not merely an agent or representative of historical influences or prior causes; he, not those causes, is therefore responsible for his action. The famous physicist Erwin Schrodinger (1944) has given the following crisp summary of the matter:

(1) My body functions as a pure mechanism according to the laws of nature.
(2) Yet I know, by incontrovertible direct experience, that I am directing its motions, of which I foresee the effects, that may be fateful and all-important, in which case I feel and take full responsibility for them.

The only possible inference from these two facts is, I think, that I ... am the person, if any, who controls the 'motion of the atoms' according to the laws of nature.[1]

There are still questions that need answers. The deterministic view asserts that all behavior is in principle predictable. It states that if we have all the relevant information about the person and his situation, we will be able to predict his action. We will see then, it is supposed, that a particular action by that person in those circumstances is inevitable. Actually, of course, the predictability of people's behavior, given the necessary information, is not just a theoretical possibility, but a constant in our lives. I am confident that my son will show up for dinner, I know enough about my friend to predict how he will vote, and so on. These predictions are not infallible, but they can approach certainty. Let us assume in the given cases that these predictions are confirmed. Can one call the resulting actions products of a free choice? Does the theoretical inevitability and predictability of any action mean that what we call "choice" is meaningless?

We can consider the totality of information that we use to predict the individual's action to represent the totality of the psychological conditions that determine his choices and his action. We ask, then, is this individual other than, more than, a transmitter of these conditions and constraints as they act upon him? But this question is misleading. It prejudices and misstates the facts. For these conditions do not act upon him. They are him. They constitute who he is. They are expressed in what he wants to do. He acts as he does in the given circumstances not because these psychological conditions cause him to do so, but because, though a product of causes, he is who he is. He owes nothing to these prior causes and conditions in choosing his actions. He has no obligation to represent them, that representation is already accomplished in his present existence. He is no more under the necessity to transmit or satisfy the causes or conditions of his nature than he is to live up to the laws of physics; he cannot do otherwise. But now we are also able to define the limits of his freedom. He is free to do what he wants, but he is not free to be someone else, someone with different beliefs, different feelings and desires than those that are presently his. In this way, therefore, what we can choose is limited and it is at this point that an unbridgeable gap appears between the determinist and the one who believes in the stronger version of free will.

The question of free will in the stronger sense or the sense of self-transcendence has often been considered in the form of a seemingly simple question: could that person have done something other than what he did? One can see at once that the question is not so simple and might easily be answered either way. The serious determinist would answer, "No, what he did, given who he was, evidently seemed to him the thing to do and, barring some change in him or his situation, he will not see it at that moment any other way." But the contrary answer, "Of course he could have done something other than what he did, everyone knows that," would be given by almost anyone else. That would be the answer given by common sense. It would be given even by the doting parent of an innocently misbehaving child. How else to teach or correct? That answer would certainly be given, also, by the moralist, who might add, how else could one make a judgment of anyone's behavior.

The fact is of course that the question, "Could that person have done something other than what he did?" does not permit a simple "yes" or "no" answer. It cannot be answered that simply on account of an ambiguity in its presentation. Imagine the following example. A brilliant young chess master, Richard, is playing an exhibition game with his elderly and long retired, but much revered former teacher. When Richard loses the game quickly, a friend of his, standing nearby, expresses puzzlement, saying, "I don't understand. You could have won that game easily." Richard answers, "No, I couldn't do that. It would humiliate him." We understand then that Richard and his friend use "could" in different ways. When the friend says "You could have won" he is thinking of Richard's technical capability.

But Richard's reply uses "couldn't" quite differently. He refers not to a technical incapability, but to his unwillingness to win. It is interesting that one can see the ambiguity of the question, "Could that person have done something other than what he did?" by imagining it to be asked in two different ways. It might be asked as the friend meant it, in an impersonal way, "Could he have *done* something else?" referring only to his technical capability, or it might be asked in a personal way, "Could *he* have done something else?" referring emphatically to Richard. Spoken the first way, with no reference to the mind and the wishes of a particular person, it is easy to imagine action other than what was done. But when the question refers clearly to this particular person, whose attitudes we know, we can understand, even predict, what he will want and choose to do and we will say, "No, being Richard, he could not have done otherwise." Indeed, if we try to imagine him deliberately winning the chess game at the cost of humiliating his teacher, we realize quickly that we are not imagining Richard, but someone else. Of course he could have done otherwise if he had wanted to, but being who he was, he could not have wanted to. We come again to the definition of our freedom of choice and its limits. We are free to do what we want, but we are not free to choose who we are.

Note

1 Schrodinger's remarks were called to my attention in a lecture by the neuroscientist Dr. Scott Kelso.

References

Farber, L. H. (1966) *The ways of the will*. New York: Basic Books.
Goldstein, K. & Martin, S. (1941) Abstract and concrete behavior: an experimental study with special tests. *Psychological monographs*, *53*(2).
Knight, R. P. (1954) Determinism, 'freedom' and psychotherapy. In R. P. Knight & C. R. Friedman (Eds)., *Psychoanalytic Psychiatry and Psychology: Clinical and Theoretical Papers*. Madison, CT: International Universities Press.
May, R. (1966) The problem of will and intentionality in psychoanalysis. *Contemporary Psychoanalysis, 3*, 55–70.
Schrodinger, E. (1944) *What is life?* Cambridge: Cambridge University Press.
Wheelis, A. (1956) Will and psychoanalysis. *Journal of the American Psychoanalytic Association, 4*, 285–303.

Chapter 6

Neurotic styles

I want to consider here, more deliberately and systematically than in Chapter 2, the self-protective compromises and curtailments of autonomy and personal responsibility in the familiar neurotic conditions. Compromises and curtailments of that kind are in fact evident in all those conditions, often integral to character, and there is no doubt that they mitigate or avert the anxiety of internal conflict. In psychoanalysis the restrictions of subjective life that forestall that kind of anxiety are called defenses. Indeed, what we see in clinical work is not so much anxiety as the ways in which anxiety is avoided or mitigated, that is, defenses. I am proposing here that all the various neurotic defense modes ultimately constitute different forms of curtailment of personal autonomy and responsibility for action. It seems on its face a plausible enough idea. If, as I suggested at the beginning of this book, awareness of one's own autonomy and personal responsibility for what one does and thinks are conditions for internal conflict and its anxiety, one might suppose that curtailing this awareness would be a condition for the forestalling or dispelling of that anxiety.

Let me start with some clarification of the process of defense itself. It is the self-protective process, originally inferred by Freud from its effects, in which anxiety is averted by the suppression of mental contents or dispositions that are intolerable to the person. It has been thought in psychoanalysis that this process operates through the action of defense "mechanisms" (repression, projection, etc). But the conception of the defense mechanisms, as well as the collection of mechanisms itself, has been full of problems. It is an admittedly haphazard collection, accumulated over the years on the basis of clinical observations, often unclear in their operation and without relation to one another or the individual's psychology as a whole. Apart from that, and more important, these psychological mechanisms are thought to work more or less independently and unconsciously, agencies operating without significant participation by the conscious activity of the person. That omission of the individual's conscious, though not self-conscious, activity, particularly of thought and speech, in the self-protective forestalling or mitigating of the anxiety of internal conflict is refuted by commonplace observation. Conscious, purposeful, though, again, unknowing of its purpose, mental activity, including speech, is central to the defense process. It is the process of self-deception. When, for example, a hypomanic young woman says, more loudly and emphatically than with conviction, "I was gorgeous last night!" the utterance itself is not merely a reflection of an unconscious defense, but is itself an unknowing defensive effort.

Some time ago I introduced a different conception of the defense process (Shapiro 1965, 1999). It is a conception based on a formal examination of neurotic conditions, that is, the ways of thinking, modes of action and qualities of subjective experience respectively characteristic of them. It is a conception of how the active, conscious, neurotic person works as opposed to a picture of how that person has been thought to be moved and restrained by various internal forces and agencies. It is, in short, an examination of neurotic ways of being, or styles, in contrast to the particular conflicts by which the various neurotic conditions had previously been known. Any style or way of being, and especially neurotic ones, while they may be expressive or adaptive, are necessarily also limiting or restrictive. It was said of George Bernard Shaw, I think by Max Beerbohm, that he saw right through the surface of people and things, but in doing so, of course, missed what was on the surface itself and was obvious to everyone else. The ways of being that are characteristic of neurotic conditions, particularly the styles of thinking and acting, are especially restrictive. That is, they limit and curtail subjective experience, in particular self-awareness, in various degrees and in different ways and, as we shall see, limit and dilute the experience of personal responsibility for what is said and done. One might say that these restrictive styles—I shall give examples in a moment—curtail and dim in those ways the brightness of the individual's experience of his own presence in the world. In that way, limiting subjective life within certain boundaries, they soften the effects of internal conflict and mitigate or forestall anxiety. Neurotic styles are, it is true, also adaptive. They are often associated, in fact, with an overdevelopment of certain narrow capabilities: thus, the productiveness of the compulsive, the engaging spontaneity of the hysteric, the quickness of decision of the psychopath, even the acute, if biased, perceptiveness of the paranoid. Each of these hypertrophied capabilities is associated with and, as it were, recompenses for the limitations and restrictions of subjective life. The driven productiveness of the compulsive person, for example, is inseparable from the restriction of his spontaneity. It is worth noting that the well-known confluence of subjective restrictions and adaptive advantages in the various neurotic conditions is easily understood from the standpoint of neurotic styles, but awkward to explain in terms of the traditional "mechanisms." These limitations and restrictions of subjective life characteristic of the various neurotic styles accomplish the effects otherwise credited to the defense mechanisms.

Regarded in this way, we can identify two loose categories of neurotic personality. There are those individuals characterized by rigid styles, so called because they live with great deliberateness, conscious of what they should do, how they should be, according to self-imposed rules. These people are therefore much concerned with self-control and general self-mastery. Diagnostically, this group includes primarily obsessive-compulsive, but also paranoid characters of various degrees of severity. The second category includes people who, if anything, seem to avoid reflective deliberateness of action. They react more immediately and easily, passively in the sense of relatively quick and unfiltered response to the provocative or forceful event or person or opportunity. In that way they can seem simply spontaneous or impetuous, though sometimes in a slightly driven way. This group includes theatrical, flighty or impressionable people of hysterical personality and, also, other more passive or impulsive individuals.

All these restrictive neurotic styles, both rigid and passively reactive ones, are derivatives of childhood modes of action that carry the limited sense of responsibility that we associate with childhood. The infant who grabs the rattle because it is there or the young child who insists on sitting in the same chair because it is the place to sit are responding to an external provocation or executing a fixed internal program, in this case a memory. In that sense they are not making reflective and deliberate choices that would carry a clear sense of personal responsibility, although those activities surely constitute the germs of agency. Only with further development are these modes gradually superseded by more reasoned aims and a more actively searching self-direction. But passively reactive and rigid modes of diminished sense of personal choice and responsibility have not disappeared in adults. They remain very much within the adult repertoire. When conflict and anxiety threaten seriously in the course of child development, the development of personality will tend toward ways that forestall it. That anxiety-forestalling development, or defense style, takes the form of a reliance on, and overdevelopment of, these early rigid and passive modes that are manifest in familiar neurotic syndromes.

Although these two groups may seem quite disparate descriptively, and in a general way they are disparate behaviorally, they are not the polar opposites they might seem. All neurotic styles have much in common, far more than may be immediately apparent. At the very least, as their respective descriptions indicate—in the one case leaning on internal rules for direction and avoidance of spontaneity, in the other leaning on external agents for direction and avoidance of deliberateness—these two categories have in common that curtailment of autonomous direction and full self-expression. The most obvious case is the obsessive-compulsive style. Consider the following example.

An obsessive man sits down in a restaurant with a friend. He examines the menu and after a short time looks distressed and uncomfortable. His friend asks him what he wants to order, but he answers irritably, "I don't know what I want." He is anxious and irritated because he feels he cannot make a choice. The decision that is so simple for his friend, who needs only to see what looks good to know what he wants, is one that he does not dare to make. Whereas his friend needs only to look at the menu, this man turns inward. He asks himself what he should have, what would be the right thing to have. In this way he consults self-imposed rules or standards—what would be healthier, what might not be available again, what is cheaper, and so forth—trying to find an objective answer that would be decisive. It is not the practical consequences of a mistaken choice that he is afraid of; the consequences would be trivial. It is the assertion of his own authority, the act and the responsibility of making a choice simply on the basis of his personal wish. Finally, when he finds a rule he can apply and whose authority seems decisive, he is relieved. He chooses and is relieved, but he cannot feel that his choice wholly expresses his wishes. He cannot confidently vouch for his own choice; it is at best a compromise.

This man avoids the anxiety of a personal choice by diverting responsibility for it to the quasi-moral authority of rules that feels superior to his own. Let us imagine that this diversion of responsibility is more continuous than an occasional episode like this one, that he not only dispels anxiety in this way but, more generally, forestalls it by a more or less constant awareness of and compliance with what he thinks he should do according to this or that principle. Or, in a more economical version of the style, that in much of his living he simply sticks to routine, that what he has done before or what he does regularly acquires its own authority and where routines are available they make articulated "I should" imperatives unnecessary. Perhaps specific reminders of what he should do or think are also superfluous in matters of action or opinion that have, like dogma, in some way acquired the imprimatur of external authority and are therefore right and uncontested. In such ways obsessive-compulsive people may greatly reduce the anxious occasions that require personal choices, choices for which they feel fully responsible. There is a psychological cost, of course. Their personal freedom is to that extent lost; they are only the executive officers of their own activity.

There is, however, an important exception to this picture. There are transgressions. No one, however conscientious in this way, however rigid and dogmatic—or, rather, because they are conscientious in this way, not out of conviction, but in obedience to rules—does all that they think they should or abstains consistently from what they shouldn't. Inasmuch as these "should"s and "should not"s carry some moral authority, transgressions will be followed by self-reproaches and shame. But they are likely to be regarded as lapses, particular failures, or aberrations; responsibility is assigned to weakness, laziness, inertia, "something infantile in me," but not really "me." The transgression is experienced as shameful, perhaps as deserving even of severe and continued punishment, but is still not experienced as an expression of the person's genuine wish or intention or in that way as fully owned or expressive of himself.

In many ways the paranoid character is an exaggeration of the compulsive, more rigid and therefore less stable. Paranoid people, also, live under the sway of authoritative images and quasi-moral standards. The emulation of those images and satisfaction of those standards (be strong, self-confident, don't give in to oneself or others) requires of them an even more rigid and self-conscious effort at self-mastery. Their alienation from much of their own subjective life is consequently more radical. The effort to be strong and self-confident, to be unfazed by challenge, shows itself, for example, in a haughty, even arrogant, but plainly hollow, knowingness. Thus, a paranoid man, arriving at the office of a psychotherapist for the first time, says, loftily, "Of course, this is all being recorded. That's alright, I don't mind" (there was no recording device).

The fragility and absence of conviction in this haughtiness shows itself in the paranoid person's extreme sensitivity to slights or indignities, particularly at the hands of those of superior rank. Such slights are regularly perceived by the individual as attempts by them to diminish him and they are experienced as humiliations. Hence paranoid people live, to various degrees, in a state of alertness and readiness to answer such attempts, to repair their dignity with indignation, sometimes with outrage. It is a state of mobilization against the external threat of humiliation, in which rigidity is, as it were, tightened into a fixed defensiveness. That subjective mobilization is often focused on an admired, perhaps grudgingly admired, figure. An acute sensitivity is thus transformed into an intensely focused and exigent attention. The object of that focus, the target, is experienced by the paranoid person as the source of his shame and humiliation and as bearing the responsibility for them or, rather, for the defensive reaction they require.

Consider the following much condensed example.

An accountant in his forties makes a declaration on his first visit to a psychotherapist, stating that he thinks very little of psychotherapy or psychotherapists or, in general, the people who go to psychotherapy. He himself, he says, has come only on account of a vocational problem, a job decision. His no-nonsense condescension already bespoke a readiness to answer any slight at the hands of the therapist. He was often angry at his bosses, especially so on this day. He denounced them loudly and furiously:

> *Patient:* The old fools!... senile! ... they can't let a young, creative person get ahead! ...

He continued at length, feeding his anger with derisive accounts of his superiors' mistakes and failings.

> *Therapist:* It sounds like something happened.

After a few moments the patient's manner softened. He became quiet, shamefaced. He answered hesitantly and with difficulty, but seeming more genuine than before.

> *Patient:* I asked (the boss) if he would have lunch with me ... (after a pause) ... he said he was too busy.

Immediately after saying this, he resumed his loud denunciations of his superiors.

Patient: They're not gonna make me jump through their hoops . . . they're senile, incompetent . . .

The momentary glimpse of this man's eagerness to be accepted by his boss, an eagerness that was humiliating and repugnant to him, shows us again how artificial and without conviction his arrogance and, indeed, his worked-up outrage was. We are also reminded here of a difference between obsessive-compulsive and paranoid people in their respective assignments of responsibility for wishes or actions that are repugnant to them. The obsessive-compulsive person regards his transgression as a shameful, but particular failure, an almost alien defect of his character, a lapse or a weakness, but not something really expressive of him, not something for which he is fully responsible. The more rigid, defensively mobilized, paranoid person experiences not simply shame at some deficiency of his own character, but humiliation for which an external agent is the responsible source ("they're not gonna make me . . .").

In some respects the curtailment of autonomous action and the sense of its ownership may be less obvious in the case of hysterical character than the rigid obsessive-compulsive or paranoid. The spontaneity of these individuals may lend them the look of free, expressive spirits, quite different from the stilted compulsive or paranoid person. That impression of freedom would be mistaken, but in an interesting way. The linguist Robin T. Lakoff (1977) has pointed out that the usual picture of hysterical character is virtually identical to a particular, now old fashioned, image of femininity. That image is marked particularly by an avoidance of any assertion of personal authority in what is said or done, to the point of a general avoidance of deliberateness or the appearance of deliberateness. In speech, as Lakoff has pointed out, this is an image of women characterized by hesitancy and vagueness ("Isn't it late-ish?"). More generally, it is a picture of an unreflective flightiness, a somewhat theatrical spontaneity or responsiveness, and suggestibility. While all this describes, as Lakoff says, a certain image of femininity, these personality features are of course by no means limited to women. It is assuredly not a picture of contemporary women, but of an anxiety-forestalling neurotic style. It is a picture of self-protective disavowal of personal authority by people who, for reasons of their history, feel little authority to begin with and do not dare exercise what little they do feel. One such person, who frequently softened her speech with childlike expressions ("grumpy," "flibberty-gibberty") recoiled from an unusually assertive opinion in a psychotherapy session with the remark, "I hope this (psychotherapy) isn't going to make me into a tough New Yorker."

Hysterics' diminished sense of their own authority, and self-protective disavowal of what authority they feel, has its complement in an overestimation of the authority of others. To one who feels small, others look large. Hence, their characteristic suggestibility. But the effect is more general and deeper than suggestibility. The unreserved immediacy of their reactiveness to what or who is there endows that external figure or situation with special evocative power. That is what is meant by hysterics' assertion that they are directed in life by their emotions, that is, by their emotional reactions, presumed to be more or less irresistible, to the external figure. The magnetism or impact of that figure or event, as it is experienced, gives some basis to the individual's sense that the responsibility for their action is at least shared by what evokes it. Thus these people are, more easily than most, intimidated by the bully, more stirred by the romantic figure, more quickly swayed by the charismatic leader, and very likely more easily hypnotized.

All the same, this general picture of disavowed authority and responsibility, like any self-protective, anxiety-forestalling style, is not necessarily consistent, and the naive and accommodating manner of a hysterical person may be interrupted by surprisingly acute perceptions and remarks. It reminds us of a fundamental fact that holds for all the various ways in which people avoid anxiety by the diminishing of their experience of themselves. That diminishment is based on self-deception; it is never completely consistent, never the whole story of a personality. The guarded person, in a comfortable setting, can laugh at a joke; the stiff, businesslike figure might relax and be playful with his little girl; the flighty one, usually not taken seriously by herself or others, when provoked, delivers a sharp, thoughtful political opinion.

Consider the following exchange from the psychotherapy of a 34-year-old woman, an actor. She was, in the way of people of hysterical makeup, a somewhat flighty and suggestible, though charming, person, given to mildly dramatic exaggerations of her feelings. She was also more intelligent than her initial impression might suggest. On this occasion she was obviously upset when she arrived at the therapist's office.

Patient: (loudly, excitedly) I'm superneurotic! I know it! superneurotic! I've got to stop it! If I don't, I'll ruin my marriage! . . .

When the therapist looked at her questioningly, she explained. Her husband is the director in a small theater group to which she also belongs. He is much admired by the members of this group, especially, apparently, by several attractive young women who gather around him. She said that she has witnessed this scene more than once and it makes her jealous and upset. She has complained several times to her husband about the situation and made her upset known to him, but to no effect. On the contrary, he has told her repeatedly and firmly that the situation is simply unavoidable, given the nature of his work. These are people he has to work with, he says, adding that she must realize this and get over her jealousy.

Patient: (overwrought and emphatic) I'm jealous of his work! He says I'm jealous of his work, and he's right! He's right! It's superneurotic! I've got to get over it! I've got to! . . . (looking urgently at the therapist) It's his work!

Therapist: You make the point again that it's his work and he can't avoid it.

She seemed taken aback by this comment and was silent, thinking, for a few moments, then,

Patient: (quieter, voice deeper, no longer sounding desperate) Of course not. He loves every minute of it. I've seen it.

This woman had seen with her own eyes, and more than once, her husband's enjoyment and encouragement of his admiring female fans, yet it did not occur to her spontaneously that his claim of innocence was untenable. On the contrary, she tried to reinforce his claim to herself repeatedly. The picture of her personality suggests some explanation. She was a person who felt little personal authority. She was not accustomed to, normally did not dare to, regard her husband or what he said critically or objectively. In that way she kept her place, which was to be likable, attractive, lively, perhaps even appealingly childlike in her manner ("I'm superneurotic!"). She did not dare to take herself or what she thought and saw seriously. She did not treat what she saw with the respect she gave to her husband's views. In all of this one can see a self-protective avoidance of personal responsibility for judgment and its assignment to him. It is interesting to note, though, that she was unable to present her husband's view with real conviction, despite her exaggerated emphasis. Her initial statement of her husband's claim ("He says . . .") was an acceptance, not a genuine judgment.

An avoidance of thoughtful, deliberate action and a corresponding externalization of responsibility for what is said and done is still more striking in more impulsive characters, especially in the extreme case of psychopathic individuals. Spur-of-the-moment action is largely opportunistic, triggered more by the situation that tempts or provokes the individual than the strength of any stable and existing aims, let alone internal deliberations. Accordingly, these people are well known for the flat assignment of responsibility for their action to the external person or situation that provokes it ("She pushed my buttons," "It was just laying there," "He resisted"). It is well known, also, that this diminished sense of personal responsibility for action is associated with a correspondingly diminished anxiety. These are men and women of action.

I suggested at the beginning of this chapter that what we actually see in neurotic individuals is not so much the anxiety of internal conflict as the ways in which that anxiety is avoided. Those self-protective ways vary greatly of course, but since they have a common aim, it is not remarkable that they should also have a common fundamental means. It seems that Kaiser's early observation that his patients did not wholly believe in, did not feel fully responsible for, what they said and did, was not only justified, but has a larger significance. What we find in the kinds of neurotic individuals we have considered is not only an incompleteness or a distortion of self-expression, but an avoidance and curtailment of it toward the end of forestalling or mitigating anxiety. That is, serving the ends that have been credited to the defense mechanisms. These anxiety-forestalling compromises and curtailments of self-expression are much more general in their effects than the suppression or inhibition of particular wishes or fantasies. They are not simply suppressive or inhibitory reactions. Their curtailment of self-expression is a product of the development and, to a certain extent, the individual cultivation, of a style. It is a limiting, though sometimes highly refined and frequently adaptive, way of being. In the most general terms, it is the individual's retreat, relying on rigid or passively reactive ways, from autonomous action and judgment and their full experience. The particular symptoms or symptomatic traits that we see clinically, the obsessions in some, the theatrics in others, the suspicions in still others, are no more than extensions and repercussions of that retreat.

References

Lakoff, R. T. (1977) Women's language. *Language and Style, X*(4), 222–247.
Shapiro, D. (1965, 1999) *Neurotic styles.* New York: Basic Books.
Shapiro, D. (2000) *Dynamics of character.* New York: Basic Books.

Chapter 7
Schizophrenia

It is best to begin a psychological discussion of schizophrenia by confronting the question of its biological origins. I take for granted that all clinical conditions, all kinds of personality, indeed our human psychology altogether, have origins in biology and our genetic makeup. We speak, we do not bark. Those genetic origins are in no way inconsistent with—on the contrary, they evidently imply—the emergence of mind and specifically of subjective life with dynamics and principles of its own. There is no reason to doubt the existence of some genetic feature, as yet unidentified, presumably of a sort that influences the forms of cognition in some general ways that constitute a vulnerability of normal cognitive function. Such a vulnerability would predispose the individual to the processes and ultimately the symptoms of schizophrenia in circumstances that would impact others differently. By vulnerability I mean that individuals retreat psychologically under stress, as they advance, in the ways that are already laid down and are open to them. It seems entirely feasible to me that careful study, particularly of the general forms of schizophrenic cognition, should contribute to the ultimate identification of those genetic features. However, as schizophrenia researcher Philip Holzman (1995), who seems to share that expectation, warns, "new technologies cannot unlock the secrets of pathophysiology and etiology by leaping from the molar behavior of symptoms to the molecular level of neurotransmitters and neuromorphology."

The early theoretical efforts to understand schizophrenia as a product and residue of childhood family dynamics, such as the "double bind" hypothesis of the mother-child relationship (Bateson, et al., 1969), that were once widely considered, are no longer of great interest. It is not only that they have not been supported by developmental evidence. More important, they have been displaced by the recognition that schizophrenia is above all a pathology of cognition, a thought disorder. That conception of schizophrenia as a thought disorder, in turn, is now widely assumed to be a more or less direct product of some biological dysfunction of genetic origin. Interest in theories of a psychological origin or basis of schizophrenia, particularly those that posit an origin in the family dynamics of childhood, has accordingly diminished. McGhie and Chapman (1961), for example, although psychoanalytical in their general view, reject the idea of schizophrenia as a product of psychological dynamics of the traditional psychoanalytic kind, insisting that the condition has to do with a problem of the "mental apparatus," by which they presumably mean biological factors. They are certainly justified in their rejection of traditional family dynamics as an explanation of schizophrenic symptoms. However, a different kind of psychological dynamics, a dynamics of the formal aspects of personality or character offers exactly that kind of insight into the varieties of cognitive modes and their relationships with kinds of psychopathology that the older dynamics did not. The formal aspects of the pathological character, the character style, are in effect a bridge connecting the individual's mode of cognition with the nature of his symptoms. It is clear, in other words, that the quality of cognition is not exempt from the formal psychological dynamics of the individual as a whole, and that cognitive styles are in fact integral to every form of psychopathology. Thus we recognize that the dogmatic thinking of the compulsive person is expressive of his rigidly conscientious, internal rule directed ("I should . . .") way of being, or that the vagueness and suggestibility of the hysteric's thinking is a symptomatic expression of a general inhibition of personal authority. As we shall see, the exacerbation of formal cognitive limitations such as these—we shall consider certain kinds of rigidity in particular—results at a certain point, for some vulnerable individuals, though not for all, in significant qualitative changes in mode of thought and relation to external reality, changes that are definitive of schizophrenia.

We have been concerned in this book with the weakening or retreat of the individual from the experience of autonomous direction of personal action, including thought and attention, and from the corresponding sense of responsibility for that action. We have seen such a diminishment of responsibility to be self-protective in its muting or forestalling of the anxiety that is sometimes entailed in autonomous action and judgment. In the case of neurotic conditions, a self-protective retreat of this sort takes the form of a special reliance on adult forms of developmentally early modes of activity and self-direction in which the experience of personal responsibility is intrinsically lacking or faint. The first of these modes is a rigid kind of self-direction in which the person surrenders direction to internal rules, searching for what he "should" do; the second is a relatively unreflective, sometimes helpless reactiveness in which direction is in effect surrendered to external demands or provocations. Each of these modes of action or thought diminishes the individual's autonomy or freedom of thought or action and therefore his experience of responsibility for what he does or for the judgments he makes. The experience of personal choice is diminished, in the one case by obedience to the authority of inner rules ("I should"), in the other case by unreflective compliance with external promptings or demands. Each of these modes may also be described as a limitation of normal volitional action. In schizophrenia, this sort of limitation of volitional action, including the volitional direction of thought and attention, takes radical forms. I shall review some of the considerable evidence for this radical effect as well as whether it can be considered to have a self-protective aim, as it has in the case of neurotic conditions.

There is widespread agreement that a central feature, many consider it to be the central feature, of schizophrenia is thought disorder. Critical to the definition of that thought disorder, manifest in a wide variety of settings and kinds of behavior, there appears consistently to be a loss of volitional control and direction of thought and attention—I shall illustrate this in a moment. We may add that where there is a loss of volitional control and direction, there must also be a loss of a sense of agency or responsibility for its result. There is great variation, of course, both in individuals on different occasions and between individuals of one kind and another. Thus, loss of volitional control of attention is generally less in nonacute paranoid schizophrenics. But the finding is essentially consistent. Clinical observers, experimenters, and psychological testers describe the phenomenon in much the same language. Psychological testers, for example, speak of "difficulties with attentional focusing, controlling and filtering irrelevant associations" (Kleiger & Khadivi 2015). I recall from my own early testing experience that a special failure of an executive kind of sustained or flexible concentration, as compared with a more passive registration, was expected of schizophrenic patients. Clinical observers of schizophrenic patients—the important work of McGhie and Chapman is exemplary—report in patient after patient distractibility and an inability to focus or direct attention voluntarily. "Everything seems to grip my attention," says one patient; "I am distracted and forget what I was saying," says another (p. 104). McGhie and Chapman report patients also being captured by the sounds of words and word fragments and losing their point as they speak. They, and others, ascribe this distractibility to an inadequacy of a selective filtering process that would inhibit attention to irrelevant stimuli. One wonders, though, if the positing of a special, filtering process or agency is not superfluous, akin to the assumption of a special capacity for delay of satisfaction, since a normal development of objective interests or goals and their attendant volitional focusing of attention would itself accomplish such a selection.

At any rate, McGhie and Chapman also make it plain that the inability to direct attention at will or sustain it in a given direction is responsible for the peculiarities of schizophrenic language use. The same inability to sustain purposeful focus, or distractibility, is manifest in the "loose" associations, "cognitive slippage" (Meehl 1962) or tangential thoughts common in schizophrenic patients that derail a train of thought into irrelevant connections or even word sounds.

An example is cited by Bleuler:

> A hebephrenic wants to sign her name to a letter as usual: 'B. Graf.' She writes 'Gra' and then a word comes to her mind; she corrects the 'a' to an 'o' and adds a double 's' making Gross, and then repeats this twice ... the patient thus loses himself in insignificant side associations ...
>
> (Rapaport 1951)

The investigator, Frith (1987), refers to schizophrenic speech disorders as "a problem in the generation of willed intentions." Interestingly, he distinguishes between stimulus-driven action—that is, the schizophrenic's immediate reaction to a stimulus—in which Frith finds no impairment, and the impaired action normally directed according to internal goals. The distinction is consistent with that recalled above from my personal testing experience. Frith's distinction and its location of the problem specifically in the failure of the purposeful self-direction that organizes thought and perception into relevant focus may receive some indirect support or confirmation from an observation sometimes made by those who have worked in mental hospitals, especially in the days before psychoactive medication. It has been noted that the general functioning of even chronic schizophrenics improves markedly when some specific purpose is imposed or at least offered by external circumstance or deliberate arrangement (Todman, 2003). Hospital workers are familiar with the surprisingly positive response of those patients to minor emergencies or special events that call for activity of a sort whose direction is prescribed. Dance therapy, simple ball playing, movement therapy all produce similar results, although, of course, only temporarily.

The phenomena of weakened self-direction and control of attention are similar in the matter of perception. The corresponding magnetism of particular stimuli is evident. Thus, Matussek (1987) states that the schizophrenic is "held captive" by an isolated object. Sass (1992), likewise, describes a passive and unfocused fixation, a prolonged staring, in which the schizophrenic loses himself in the object. Others, for example Cutting and Dunne (1989), report patients being captivated by bright colors, these being sometimes described as luminous or psychedelic to the schizophrenic. McGhie and Chapman (1969) also report a schizophrenic patient's heightened response to sound experience: "noises all seem to be louder than they were before . . . it makes it difficult to keep your mind on something when . . . you can't help listening" (p. 52). The schizophrenic hyperawareness of bodily sensations is thought to be a manifestation of a similar captivation by isolated stimuli. Again, it is easy to understand this phenomenon as the effect, not of an absent or lacking inhibitory agency or filter, but of a faltering or inadequate volitional directedness of purposeful attention. It has been said of, I believe, Japanese painters that they will sometimes bend over and look at the scene upside down through their legs thus diminishing their focus on objects in order to intensify their experience of the colors.

It is not hard to understand that the loss or diminishment of autonomous, volitional direction of attention has the effect, also, of a corresponding loss of a clear sense of a separate or objective external world. A clear picture of an external object requires not just an ability to see, but an interest and capacity to look, to focus attention on things, to direct attention purposely, deliberately, flexibly. The displacement of such an active, intentionally focused attitude by a helplessly passive one that is easily distracted, captured, and held, by fragments, often affectively significant and out of context, must entail a loss of the separate, objective external world. Thus, Renee, the patient of the Swiss psychiatrist, Sechehaye (1968), recalled, after her recovery, anxiously entering the administrator's office at the beginning of her hospitalization, and seeing "her teeth, white and even in the gleam of light . . . soon they monopolized my entire vision as if the room were nothing but teeth under a remorseless light" (p. 22). In place of a distinct, objective figure, a compelling detail of the scene imbued with her anxiety has captured her attention. It is very much the way a defensively alert paranoid schizophrenic may seize on a fragment of their surroundings, perhaps a word from the radio or a sign on the road, that is seen or heard as threatening. One such patient, for example, noticing the quiet murmur of conversation from a couple passing on the street, insisted that she had heard a sinister, hissing, "psst! psst!" directed at her.

It is worth considering, also, that the impairment of a purposeful attitude of focused, deliberate looking not only has an effect on the clarity of the external world, but is bound as well to blur the subject's sense of himself and even his experience of his own physical or kinetic activity. The schizophrenic's weakened or uncertain sense of his own physical agency is of course well known clinically in the paranoid individual's ideas, for instance, of his physical movements being directed by external "influence machines" or by others. The subject has also received extensive experimental study, with hypotheses concerning sensorimotor and cognitive cues (Synofzik, et al., 2010).

The experiences of paranoid schizophrenics, anxiously constructed around decontextualized fragments, like the more elaborate delusional ideas, are often expressed by their subjects with certainty. The individual says, "I knew at once . . ." The paranoid schizophrenic, Schreber (1955), made famous in Freud's theory of paranoia, whose case I shall return to in a moment, upon noticing a "crackling noise," recognized it at once as "undoubted divine miracles." It is a mistake to consider such experiences to be ones of genuine conviction. They are not. These ideas are not the result of looking things over, an objective view of the external world, and a confident conclusion that one has gotten it right. They are, rather, experiences largely of the subject's own internal sensations and ideas, though they may make use of external fragments. They are in essence experiences of personal revelation. Thus, a man convicted of a shooting rampage in which two people were killed says later that the divine command to kill is "not visual. It's not auditory. It's just, you realize it."[1] Bits and pieces of the external world taken from their context reveal themselves as embodiments of large anxieties and ideas.

We can say that a radical retreat from or disability of autonomous volitional control and direction of thought and attention is central to schizophrenic symptomatology. We have seen that the anxiety-forestalling styles of neurotic conditions employ adult forms of early developmental modes, reliance on internal rules or passive compliance with external suggestion, in which the experience of autonomy and responsibility, the sense of deliberateness and intentional choice, is weak. Can we say that in some, though by no means all, individuals an exacerbation of those ways of forestalling or dispelling anxiety may account for the cognitive symptoms, the thought disorder, of schizophrenia?

Consider the paranoid case. We have discussed in the previous chapter the rigidity of the nonpsychotic paranoid individual, including images and rules of what he should be and a concern with self-mastery that is more extreme and therefore less stable than the compulsive's. And we have seen how vulnerable, on that account, the paranoid person is to humiliation, to being made to feel small and ashamed, hence how sensitive, guarded, defensively mobilized against indignity he is. Let us suppose that this sensitivity, this rigidity, and the shame that it hides are further intensified, perhaps in reaction to some new external circumstance, and consider what the effects may be on cognition.

If sensitivity is greater, so must be defensive alertness. The self-protective anticipation and search for an external threat must become more exigent. The particular element in the external world that may satisfy that search increasingly commands notice. That element, seized from its context, is more easily, more immediately, recognized. The more rigid the defensive bias, the more urgent and selective the defensive search, the easier and more immediate the recognition of the confirming element. The reader may note here that this recognition of the confirming fragment can be described, as I have, in two apparently contradictory ways; on the one hand, as an active, searching attention ("seized" from its context), on the other hand, as the passively, almost helplessly captured attention ("commands notice"). But the cognitive processes described in these ways are actually not very far apart, and both descriptions are apt. An intensely selective, severely biased attention, as in a paranoid hyperalertness, is an actively searching attention only in a very limited sense, since it finds its confirming clue so easily, immediately and relatively indiscriminately. The immediacy of this kind of recognition of the anticipated and decontextualized clue weakens the normal sense of an objective situation separate from and without any special relationship to the observer.

Thus, an anxious and guarded patient enters a therapist's office for the first time. He sees at once, on the shelf at some distance, a book with the word "hypnosis" in its title. In that instant the patient, out of his anxious search, summons the idea of a threatening hypnotist in the person of the therapist. This is not a deduction; the threat is already contained in the patient's perception of the book.

As the confirming element becomes easier to discover, less and less[2] in reality is required to satisfy expectations, themselves increasingly fixed and increasingly urgent. At some point of the severity of this rigidity, the individual's critical judgment disappears. It is replaced by a direct and immediate connection between the fixed bias and an external element that satisfies it. The immediacy of that connection causes it to be experienced as compelling and to be revealed as directed at the subject, like a signal. It is at this point that the acutely paranoid person reports with "certainty" that personally threatening messages "jump out" at him from billboards and the radio. In this condition thought has become merely reactive. Instead of active, consciously intentional or deliberate judgment, instead of looking things over, preformed, stereotyped ideas are triggered by associatively significant fragments of external reality or one's own thoughts. This is the loss or suspension of executive control of attention and of an objective external world, the cognitive conditions that permit such classical symptoms of schizophrenia as looseness, confusion or tangentiality. The thought disorder is the direct result of the psychological dynamics of the individual, not the family dynamics of childhood, however developmentally important that may have been, but the formal dynamics of the adult character and cognition.

A fascinating example of these dynamics, their course and their result, is the case of paranoid schizophrenia made famous by Freud. Freud used the detailed exposition by the German jurist, Daniel Paul Schreber, of his acute (and still, at the time of writing, not completely in remission) psychotic breakdown, *Memoirs of My Nervous Illness* (1903), in developing his theory of paranoia as a defense against unconscious homosexual wishes. Schreber's primary delusion was that he was being transformed, against his will and to his horror, into a woman for purposes of sexual abuse. Initially he thought that his doctor, Dr. Flechsig, was responsible for this effect; later, he believed it was God. Schreber was the son of an orthopedic physician and authority on child development whose program demanded strict control of the child, to be enforced not only by detailed rules and instructions but also, by orthopedic appliances, for proper posture and such. Schreber was himself a man of strikingly rigid attitudes: dignified, dutiful, ascetic, highly moralistic. He described himself as "morally unblemished." At the time of an evidently destabilizing change in his official position, actually a promotion, during a period of anxious and disturbing dreams, he had, before completely waking, the "highly peculiar" thought that "it really must be rather pleasant to be a woman succumbing to intercourse." It was a thought, he says, that he "would have rejected with indignation" if he had been fully awake. Thereupon his struggle began not only against his sexual fantasies and wishes, but more generally against the undermining of his manly honor and self-control. He consulted Dr. Flechsig, whose "remarkable eloquence" at first impressed him very much, but about whom he quickly developed defensive suspicions. Once hospitalized, evidences of the effort to "degrade" him were, inevitably, immediately apparent to his increasingly defensive, rigid bias. The context of any such evidence that would deprive it of sinister meaning is disregarded. Any other point of view, any detachment or critical judgment, is excluded by the fixed necessity to identify the threat. What follows is only the unfolding of the prejudice. Thus the idea that Flechsig had "secret designs" against him "seemed confirmed" by the fact that, during a visit, Flechsig "could no longer . . . look me straight in the eye." Agitated and admitted to the hospital, he "definitely" came to realize that highly sexual "female nerves" and "voluptuousness" were being insinuated into his body in the effort, by Flechsig and with God's connivance, to transform him into a "female harlot."

It is interesting to consider the question whether arriving at such a thought, horrifying as it clearly was to this rigidly upright, moralistic man, can be considered to be anxiety-dispelling, self-protective, a defense. The question is easy to answer. One needs only to consider that the alternative to this imagined threat, the even more horrifying possibility that it protects against, is that the fantasy of becoming a "female harlot" is not a threat, but a wish. The projection, that is, the relocation of responsibility, is protective. It is worth noting, also, that in the case of paranoid schizophrenia, notwithstanding a general weakening of autonomous direction of thought and attention, a semblance of active direction is often maintained. It may include an exaggerated, even grandiose sense of comprehension.

This appears to have been the case for Schreber. He was apparently never free of delusion, but he did come to think that his transformation was God's wish and, characteristically, therefore his duty to accept.

Catatonic schizophrenia, much rarer than paranoid, also seems to emerge from severely obsessive conditions. Obsessive traits, in fact, are often conspicuous in the catatonic state itself. Numerous cases in which an obsessively perfectionistic self-scrutiny, precautionary hesitancy, and indecision are prominent are described by David Read Johnson (1984). Johnson says, in a review of eight case reports on catatonic patients, "All [treated by different therapists] show significant . . . obsessive symptoms." Of one patient, typical of the group, it is reported that she "berated herself for not being 'perfect' enough," another had attempted to "perfect himself" through physical exercise, yet another is described by his therapist as "perfectionistic, obsessional," and Johnson himself describes his patient as "almost immobilized when faced by a decision." Silvano Arieti's (1974) picture of a catatonic patient of his is consistent with this and offers a somewhat enlarged idea of its subjective experience. Arieti says of his patient, she "was afraid to make any movement. Any movement she made might be wrong." Indeed, the catatonic condition, whose most obvious and distinctive symptom is an immobilization seemingly absent of all decision ("waxy flexibility"), may easily give the impression of being an exaggeration of the kind of obsessive scrupulosity and consequent indecision that is paralyzing. Conversely, the kind of paralysis that sometimes results from severe obsessive indecision can resemble a catatonic condition.

One severely obsessive man, at the time a patient in an open psychiatric hospital, was frequently observed standing motionless for long periods on nearby street corners. He was often mistakenly assumed to be catatonic when noticed by hospital personnel at such times. In actual fact, he was not schizophrenic, but only agonizing over which way he should go. However marked the resemblance to obsessive conditions, in the case of the catatonic it is not only the degree, but the rigidity of scrupulosity that is greatly magnified. The catatonic's attitudes, of which such an outright immobilization is an expression, are dominated by rules that are far more extensive and, perhaps above all, more exacting in their scrupulousness. These self-imposed rules, generally implicit in attitudes of conscientiousness, require that no possibility, however remote, that may be harmful or wrong in some other sense, be permitted. They may be in principle relentless. If so, ultimately, no consciously intentional action can pass inspection.

Thus, Arieti says of one catatonic patient, even in the period prior to the actual catatonic state, "Every action . . . became loaded with a sense of responsibility. Every willed movement came to be seen . . . as a moral issue." Another patient "had the impression that small pieces or corpuscles were falling down on her body or from her body . . . she was afraid that her movements would cause small pieces to fall . . . it kept her in mortal fear of any movement . . ." Tahka (1993), similarly, describes a 15-year-old girl who is terrified of causing damage to (imagined) flies on the floor and will not permit any movement in the room either by herself or anyone else. "She stands . . . staring keenly at the floor and being careful not to move from the spot. Her cheeks are puffed up with saliva which she obviously cannot let herself either swallow or spit . . ."

A scrupulosity, a rule-directed conscientiousness, that is this exacting affects not only behavior, or restraint of behavior, but the formal mode of cognition in ways comparable to those I have described in the paranoid case. In other words, an increasingly rigid and relentlessly exacting scrupulosity requires an increasingly biased, selective and urgent identification of unacceptable possibilities. Horrific consequences may be conjured up by the relentlessly conscientious search. Any judgment that might find otherwise, as in considering mitigating context, fails the test of that scrupulosity. Hence normal, autonomous judgment, looking things over, is put aside, suspended. Finally, fragmentary ideas or perceptions that satisfy bias will be seized with a directness and immediacy in which the individual's active judgment has been displaced by a kind of technical reactiveness. Thus, Angyal (1950) describes a patient: "Every little movement he made assumed a cosmic significance . . . even lifting a finger or taking a step would have incalculable consequences" (p. 155). Here, much as in the case of paranoid schizophrenia, active, personal judgment, even consciously deliberate restraint, are replaced by the reflexive executing of the rules of scrupulosity, relentlessly pressed to the point of immobility. But it is not only precautionary behavior that has at this point become merely reactive. The state of immobility reflects, also, the displacement of volitional direction of attention and thought and, in that way, the general surrender of autonomy and responsibility for thought and action. This is to say, also, the surrender of that in which the person primarily experiences himself. The catatonic patient of Arieti's felt himself "solidifying." Arieti describes him as resembling "a statue of stone." We may say here that the psychological dynamics of a relentlessly rigid conscientiousness have produced in this patient a schizophrenic thought disorder.

A further, perhaps qualifying, note of significance needs to be added to this picture of schizophrenia. It has again to do with the nature of the schizophrenic's delusional experience and the mental state represented in that experience. I have made the point, referring to paranoid delusions, that the schizophrenic's expression of certainty cannot be taken at face value as genuine conviction. It seems, rather, to reflect an experience of revelation, an idea that presents itself abruptly, satisfying an unrecognized expectation, and unspoiled by any mitigating judgment of objective circumstances. Many therapists and observers have noted that actively delusional schizophrenics are often capable of conducting their lives in ways that are utterly inconsistent with the nature of their delusion. The patient who insists he is working hard as the president of the United States has no problem taking the subway into Manhattan to see his therapist. Louis Sass calls the phenomenon, aptly, "double bookkeeping." Cutting and Dunne (1989) speak of "a dual thinking process" in schizophrenia. Their report of retrospective observations by schizophrenic individuals in remission about their experience makes the point clearly: they describe six patients, each of whom recalls "the simultaneous occurrence of two separate modes of thinking." A typical observation by one of these patients: "I was in two minds, I could snap out of it if I wanted." Sechehaye's patient, Renee, puts the experience in a slightly different way, saying, of her earlier terrifying delusional experiences, "Nonetheless, I did not believe that the world would be destroyed as I believed in real facts" (p. 27).

The mutability of the schizophrenic's attitude in this respect is illustrated, also, in the following (condensed) exchange between a man in an acutely delusional paranoid state, at least initially, and his therapist. Looking very nervous and frightened, the patient is relating his terrifying experience. He says that he is being followed by his former colleagues and he has heard the threatening messages they have sent over the radio.

Therapist: You look grim.
Patient: Wouldn't you? . . . if all your friends were doing what John (his boss) wants . . . the car is bugged, the house is bugged . . . they're using recorders. . . . John is dominating everything.

Therapist:	You sound like a driver who thinks he's been speeding and every car in the mirror looks like police.
Patient:	... (more quietly, thoughtfully) You mean, even if they're bugging my house and my car, I don't have to be so worried about it? That's an idea.... Maybe I could just put it aside for a while.
Therapist:	Maybe. We'll see.
Patient:	Suppose you had done terrible things, perversions ... are you saying I shouldn't feel that way.
Therapist:	Yes, I think you shouldn't feel that way.
Patient:	What do you think about somebody who's sneaky, who's one thing in private and something completely different in public?
Therapist:	I think that's probably a person who feels ashamed of himself in private and thinks he has to hide in public.
Patient:	(more lightly) That makes sense.
Therapist:	You're thinking of dismissing the charges?
Patient:	(smiles) No, but I'm thinking of reducing them from felony to misdemeanor.

It has to be said that the more benign state of mind conveyed in the patient's last comment did not last long. The paranoid terrors were soon resurrected. Nevertheless, that this temporary change was achieved so easily also speaks of the delusion as something quite different from regular belief or conviction. The tentative change of mind ("Maybe I could just put it aside for a while") that came so easily to this paranoid person surely tells us that he had not actually *believed* in the first place, in the ordinary sense and meaning of belief, that his room was bugged, that messages were coming to him from the radio, etc. It tells us much the same as the observations and recollections, quoted above, that speak of delusion as reflective of a mental state that is an alternative to the one represented by belief or conviction. This of course is what Sechehaye's patient Renee tells us quite explicitly when she says, "I did not believe that the world would be destroyed as I believed in real facts." It is a state of mind in which the normal deliberative and objective interest in the world is suspended in favor of a relentless execution of the rigid internal requirements of scrupulosity or defensive suspicions to the point of unreality. It is a kind of short-circuiting of the normal, volitional, cognitive processes, too immediate a connection between those internal requirements and fragments of the external world, with a corresponding loss of personal agency.

We may also be reminded here of the lack of conviction that is regularly apparent in self-deception, and the uncertainty of their own reliability that individuals sometimes show in their effort to deceive themselves ("Boy, it's almost like I'm making it [the 'recovered' memory] up, but I'm not" or the subject of Chinese thought reform who says "You begin to believe all this, but it is a special kind of belief"). As I make this point, referring in this connection to the absence of genuine conviction also in those instances of self-deception, I do not mean to erase the special nature of the schizophrenic delusion or the special vulnerabilities that may dispose toward it. It is only to suggest that here, too, regular cognitive processes are not necessarily destroyed, but only out of reach.

Note

1 Reported in the *New York Times*, April 12, 2000.

References

Angyal, A. (1950) The psychodynamic process of illness and recovery in a case of catatonic schizophrenia. *Psychiatry*, *13*, 149–165.

Arieti, S. (1974) *Interpretation of schizophrenia* (2nd ed.). New York: Basic Books.

Bateson, G., Jackson, D. D., Haley, J., & Weakland, J. (1969) Toward a theory of schizophrenia. In A. H. Buss & E. H. Buss (Eds.), *Theories of Schizophrenia*. Redwood City: Atherton Press.

Bleuler, E. (1951) The basic symptoms of schizophrenia. In D. Rapaport (Ed.), *Organization and pathology of thought* (pp. 581–649). New York: Columbia University Press.

Cutting, J., & Dunne, F. (1989). Subjective experience of schizophrenia. *Schizophrenia Bulletin*, *15*(2), 217–231.

Freud, S. (1949) Psychoanlytic notes upon an autobiographical account of a case of paranoia. *Collected Papers*, vol III. Hogarth Press.

Frith, C. D. (1987). The positive and negative symptoms of schizophrenia reflect impairments in the perception and initiation of action. *Psychological Medicine*, *17*, 631–648.

Johnson, D. R. (1984) Representation of the internal world in catatonic schizophrenia. *Psychiatry*, *47*, 299–314.

Kleiger, J. H., & Khadivi, A. (2015) *Assessing psychosis: a clinician's guide*. Oxford: Routledge.

McGhie, A., & Chapman, J. (1961) Disorders of attention and perception in early schizophrenia. *British Journal of Medical Psychology, 34*, 103–116.

Meehl, P. E. (1962) Schizotaxia, schizotypy, schizophrenia. *American Psychologist, 17*, 827–838.

Sass, L. (1992) *Madness and modernism.* New York: Basic Books.

Schreber, D. P. (1955) *Memoirs of my nervous illness*, trans. Ida McAlpine and Richard Hunter, William Dawson. Cambridge, MA: Harvard University Press.

Sechehaye, M. (1968) *Autobiography of a schizophrenic girl.* New York: New American Library.

Synofzik, M., Tier, P., Leube, D. T., Schloterbeck, P., & Lindner, A. (2010) Misattributions of agency in schizophrenia are based on imprecise predictions about the consequences of one's actions. *Brain*, 262–271.

Tahka, V. (1993) *Mind and its treatment.* Madison: International Universities Press.

Chapter 8

Saying something is doing something

I want now to take up an old problem of psychoanalysis or psychoanalytically influenced therapy. It is a problem, in fact, that probably affects all kinds of "talk therapy." While it presents itself as a problem of therapeutic method, I take it up here because it embodies more general issues that are, as the reader will recognize, essentially the same ones that have been considered in previous discussions in this book. The problem concerns the nature of speech as purposeful action and the experience of responsibility for, or conviction in, what one says and does.

In all talk therapy patients are encouraged, by the opportunity that the situation provides, even if not explicitly by the therapist, to reveal themselves, to talk as freely as possible about their problems and concerns, which of course includes themselves, their own thoughts and feelings. In psychoanalysis this expectation is presented in its strongest form in the instruction to the patient not to censor or withhold anything that comes to mind, although it is understood that this expectation is never fulfilled completely, and in fact is itself inevitably a focus of conflict for the patient. The material that is thus provided by the patient, the memories, associations, narrative content that emerges is then considered to constitute the essential therapeutic material. That is, this is the material that the analyst or therapist uses or interprets in order to understand the patient and his underlying problems. What the patient provides in this way, the thoughts, associations, memories, and feelings that he or she relates, are usually taken to be, if correctly understood, like a key or a window to the patient's mind, and to express or signify the conflicts or anxieties manifest in symptoms and anomalous traits in the neurotic adult.

Psychoanalytic method, from its beginnings with Freud, has of course distinguished itself by its extraordinary close and sensitive attention to what the patient relates in this way, to his stories, to the inner feelings he reports, even to the patient's particular words, not merely to their literal meaning but, as well, to their possible metaphorical and unconscious significance. As we all know, discoveries were made by that kind of attention, previously unrecognized wishes, prohibitions, complications of the mind were revealed. But the method and kind of attention also impose a certain limitation of both therapeutic and theoretical significance. The very closeness of the analyst's or therapist's attention to the subject matter that the patient relates, the narrative content, the memories, associations, and the rest, that the patient produces, may by the very nature of its focus fail to include attention to the patient's immediate experience of his own production. That is, the analyst's or therapist's interest in the content of the patient's productions may be accompanied by neglect of the attitude, the degree of conviction, the purpose and degree and kind of interest with which the patient offers these productions. For what the patient says can be said in many different ways with many different purposes, conscious and unconscious, none of them resembling what would be conveyed by a transcript typed out on a blank page. The result of such a neglect, especially, as we shall see in the following paragraphs, of the degree of the patient's conviction and genuine interest, is likely to be an understanding of the patient's mind that is at best abstract and, for the patient, a kind of education about his own psychology and the achievement of what is commonly called an intellectual insight, without real therapeutic change.

The problem of intellectual insight, if it is that, without real change was not unknown even in the comparatively early days of psychoanalytic treatment. It was the stimulus and the main target of the major therapeutic and theoretical contribution in the 1920s and 1930s by Wilhelm Reich. At the time, of course, Reich was still a psychoanalyst, not yet involved in his fantastic psychobiological ideas. Correcting that problem and, as Reich saw it, reaching the emotional sources of the neurotic condition, was the essential aim of his therapeutic program, an aim that was emphasized repeatedly in his book *Character Analysis* (1949). As it turned out, however, the correction of the specific problem led, if not always explicitly, to a new, more general therapeutic point of view. The nature of Reich's dissatisfaction and at least a hint of the direction in which he sought its solution can be conveyed by the critical and, for its time, extraordinary clinical example he offered at the beginning of his book. It is drawn from his own work, but it refers to a patient who, though at the time of writing a patient of Reich's, had been in treatment with another analyst for some time without result. Reich says, the patient produced unconscious material uninterruptedly and was able, for instance, to present the finest details of the simple and double Oedipus complex. *I asked the patient whether he really believed what he was saying and what he had heard* (my emphasis). 'But not in the least,' he said, 'with all this I cannot help smiling inside.'

(pp. 24–25)

With this example Reich introduces his criticism of the interpretation of "content," that is, the unconscious infantile wishes and anxieties suggested by the patient's associations and dreams, when the patient's resistance, which for Reich consisted of the patient's neurotic character and characteristic attitudes, makes those interpretations ineffective. These are the interpretations that, Reich argues, fail to produce a genuine emotional response and therefore fail to effect any therapeutic change. By that route, he says, "the patient may develop a good intellectual understanding and perhaps a theoretical conviction of the correctness of the analytic work, but there is very little change." One may doubt, taking note of Reich's own example, whether a patient would in fact develop genuine conviction even about the theoretical correctness of the analytic work as a result of this kind of understanding. The more likely and, I think, more common reaction to this kind of understanding is its acceptance as plausible rather than conviction.

Reich's question, asking whether the patient actually believed what he was saying and what he had heard, may well strike the reader of his book with surprise, as it presumably did his patient. Reich is suddenly looking in a new direction. For the question reflects a significant change and expansion of the direction and scope of therapeutic attention. Before this moment, Reich's attention had evidently been directed exclusively at the ideational content, the subject matter, the associations, memories, that the patient produced. Up to this point the "unconscious material" produced by the patient may well have been regarded by Reich as a window to the patient's mind. But at this point Reich's attention broadened. He does not tell us why, and he may not have known himself. At any rate, his attention now included *the person who produced* those associations, fantasies, and memories. Specifically, Reich's attention was drawn to the patient's attitude toward what he was hearing and saying, and therefore to the patient himself as active speaker or listener. To become aware of the patient as speaker or listener in this way, speaking or listening according to his prevailing attitude, is to bring into focus a new picture of the patient. Where before he had been seen merely as a passive conduit for unconscious material, he now appears as actively, if sometimes unknowingly, purposeful in what he says and how he listens. What the patient says is no longer understood simply as a window to his mind but, rather, as what this person, for his own conscious or unconscious reasons, chooses to say. We may add, with Reich's patient in mind, what this person chooses to say with greater or less conviction and greater or less real interest.

Otto Fenichel (1990), expressing the view of classical psychoanalysis with considerable authority, says,

> When the selective conceptual goals of the ego are excluded [by the analytic instruction to say what comes to mind–DS], what is expressed is determined rather by tensions and impulses within the individual awaiting the opportunity to gain expression.
>
> (p. 24)

Fenichel's conception here is of the conscious individual as a passive or, transparent conduit for those "tensions and impulses," at least to the extent—and it is surely assumed to be possible to a considerable extent—that he can exclude the conceptual goals of the ego. The conception is basic to the assumption that the resulting ideas, associations, memories, the narrative content that emerges, constitute the therapeutic material and can, provided that it is correctly understood, provide access to the mind. Indeed, that conception of the therapeutic material and the more or less exclusive direction of attention to the ideational content produced by the patient is formalized in the traditional analytic arrangement in which the patient lies on the couch. In this arrangement, after all, the expression on the patient's face, the look in his eyes, which in normal communication are important and often essential to empathic understanding, is sacrificed by the analyst. From the standpoint of a therapeutic interest that is limited to the narrative content, however, it is not a sacrifice at all; from that standpoint, the facial expression, the patient's look, as he speaks may be no more than a distraction.

But we now know that the "conceptual goals of the ego" cannot be excluded. Fenichel's conception of what is expressed, of speech, is therefore not correct. The tensions and impulses, in his conception, are believed to seek expression on account of their own impetus and toward their own aims. It is not a plausible conception, as we have seen, of human speech or action. The implication of Reich's example, and the reality, is otherwise. Language does not leap from a person's mouth on account of its own impetus. When a person speaks, however much he may at that moment be trying to follow the analytic instruction, in effect, to act as an observer, a conduit, for mental contents that present themselves, he speaks not on account of the impetus of those contents or the feelings that prompted them or at their direction, but according to *his* aims and intentions. Not the least of those, we may imagine, often being the far from inconsiderable intention to be a cooperative patient. We know now that all behavior, including speech, is more actively directed, no speech is mere text. It is language used by a person for purposes recognized or unrecognized. In short, speech is volitional action. Saying something is doing something, in the phrase of the English philosopher, J. L. Austin (1962), and the patient is an active and responsible, if sometimes unwitting, agent of what he says.

For Reich, therefore, the therapeutic material therefore was no longer limited to the patient's ideational productions: it now included the whole of the active person; his gait, his posture, the intonation of his voice and especially, if we may go a little beyond Reich here, still in the spirit of his argument, the expression of his face and the look in his eyes—in other words, all that reflects his attitude. Thus, Reich says:

> What does that mean, 'analytic material'? The usual concept is: the patient's communications, dreams, associations, slips. True, there is often theoretical realization that the total behavior of the patient also has analytic significance, but clear-cut experiences ... show that the behavior of the patient ... (is) usually completely overlooked.
>
> (p. 29)

This is the basis for Reich's famous precept for therapists. "The how of saying things is as important 'material' ... as is what the patient says" (p. 45). To pay attention to how things are said is to pay attention to what the person is doing by saying it, and Reich's repeated emphasis in *Character Analysis* is in fact on what the patient is doing by saying what he is saying. Thus when a patient has produced "infantile material" in abundance, Reich emphasizes that he did not interpret it because the patient was "offering (it) up" merely to satisfy the analyst. When a colleague complains that a patient is silent, Reich says, "Is not the behavior itself, the silence during the hour ... 'material' enough?" Reich does not say all that I have said here, but the perspective is his and it shows itself unmistakably in his choice to open his book with that unusual question to his patient, asking "whether he really believed what he was saying and what he had heard."

The psychoanalytic or psychotherapy patient's speech is purposeful action; it can no longer be considered a transparent or neutral expressive conduit of thoughts and feelings, itself innocent of special purpose or attitude, and therefore not requiring special attention. The fact that saying something is doing something means, for example, that speech itself, not only its thought content, can be an occasion of internal conflict. We are familiar with the anxiety and inhibition that can accompany the utterance of an idea that is already conscious or consciously forming.

Consider the following example.

A middle-aged man tells his therapist of his wife's complaint that he never tells her that he loves her. He says he "cannot" do that: "I don't know why, but I can't." He says that this may be because he's not sure that he does love her. But then he says, carefully and more quietly, as though he is making an admission, that he "probably" does. After a pause, he then recalls that as a young man he told other women that he loved them, though he didn't mean it. They expected it, so he said it. But with his wife, he says with difficulty, his voice now breaking, it, that is, he, would feel "mushy," "sentimental." It should be noted that it is not only that he "cannot" say this to his wife; he could hardly utter it in the therapist's office with his wife absent.

Even the assumption that ordinary therapeutic arrangements that might otherwise be thought to provide a more or less neutral setting for ideas or feelings seeking expression, as Fenichel put it, comes into question when one realizes that it is not ideas or feelings that are seeking expression, but a person, a purposeful individual, who is, furthermore, conscious of where he is and what is expected of him. Even the patient's consciousness of being a patient, exaggerated as it often is by an expectation of self-observation of the mind's contents, as in "Yesterday I thought . . .," "I think I feel . . .," etc., dilutes the experience of those contents and the sense of their ownership, with the implied assignment of responsibility for their existence to the thoughts and feelings themselves.

Consider the following example.

A 24-year-old divorced female patient reluctantly tells her male therapist that she has had a dream about him. It is very difficult to tell him this dream, she says, or even to mention its existence, because telling it would "amplify it." The patient is struggling with the problem when, a few moments later, another thought occurs to her. She remembers that she is, after all, "a patient telling my therapist" a dream. She adds, "That makes it easier." It is no longer something she *says to the therapist*, but quite different, something she *tells the therapist about*. She has realized that she is only doing her work as a patient, reporting material. Her sense of personal responsibility for what she is about to say is diminished.

It is likely that the use of the couch has a similar effect, making formal patients' consciousness of their patient-ness, underlining their awareness that they are doing what they are expected to do, providing material, and in this, diluting their realization that what they are saying and doing is directly expressive of them. There is no doubt that being out of the listener's sight makes it easier for most people to talk about their personal lives than it would be face to face. Probably this fact justifies the arrangement for most analysts who favor it. But why is it easier? Why, for instance, do people feel less ashamed of what they have to say if they are out of the listener's sight and do not have to meet his glance? The reason must be that in this arrangement the sense of contact, of directness of communication, of seeing in the other one's eyes that he has understood, in short, the sense of responsibility for what one is saying, is diluted.

To treat speech as a neutral conduit of ideas and feelings seeking to express themselves, as Fenichel proposed, not only slights the fact of speech as volitional action. In doing so, it also slights the subjective significance of the irregularities, the idiosyncratic vagaries of the speech action, the manner, not just the content, of speech. In a practical way, for the therapist, it overlooks the great variety of conscious and unconscious aims and uses to which people put language and speech apart from simple communication of their feelings or ideas to another person. One can, in speaking, simply share ideas or feelings with another person, but one can also, without knowing it, speak for the effect on oneself ("I must end this relationship!"). One can speak to express what he feels and believes, but one can also express what he only thinks he feels and believes, or what he thinks he should feel and believe, or is trying to persuade himself to feel or believe. One can express what he is deeply interested in or offer dutifully what he thinks the listener is interested in. Or one can speak to prove something or show something to someone else or to oneself without realizing that one is doing so. And so on.

The communicative intention of what is said, beyond its literal content, that is, to warn, to teach, etc., was called by the philosopher J. L. Austin (1962) its illocutionary force. Commonly, the illocutionary force of a speech act, what the speaker is doing by saying what he is saying, is simply expressive of what he means and is easily, if tacitly, understood by the listener. Thus, the speaker is giving, and means to give, a warning, or a promise, or to teach or share an experience, or some such, and the listener understands that. However, in some speech the illocutionary force is not so clear. This is especially so in speech in which the speaker is not fully behind the conscious intention of what he is saying. That is, when he is not fully behind what he is doing, or consciously trying to do, by saying what he is saying. This is specifically the case in self-deceptive speech. The illocutionary force of his utterance is, as a result, experienced by the listener as somewhat artificial or unconvincing, blurred by the existence of some contrary feeling or belief whose nature can only be inferred. In other words, here again we see evidence of internal conflict, not necessarily in what is said, but in the act of saying it. Regarding speech in this way presents us with a kind of dynamics inherent in speech action. I shall give some examples in a moment.

It is often, and rightly, recommended to psychotherapists to pay special attention in their work to the "here and now" in the therapeutic situation, but it is a recommendation that is highly ambiguous. For example, it is sometimes understood as referring only to the patient's present relationship with the therapist or to other current subjects as they appear in the narrative content. But the precept has its clearest meaning and application in attention to the dynamics of the patient's action at the present moment, which is his speech action. It is in this action, in doing what he is doing by saying what he is saying, that he attempts to forestall or dispel whatever anxiety, though mostly unarticulated and at the moment unknown to him, signals its presence by some subjective discomfort. This anxiety-forestalling or dispelling action is by no means limited to speech consisting of a single sentence or two. It may easily consist of lengthy and continuing presentations.

Consider the following examples.

> A 35-year-old man's expressions to his psychotherapist of unhappiness about his wife and his marriage have become repetitious and, it seems, unnecessarily detailed. She is, he says, interested only in shopping and spending money, perpetually dissatisfied and angrily complaining, about their apartment, his work schedule, the children, and so forth. It's impossible, he says, to live this way. He frequently adds, though, that he could not leave, on account of his attachment to their children. His complaints

are not so remarkable in themselves; he seems sincere and the stories he tells seem believable, but they are repeated in session after session and always said with a certain emphatic earnestness. He often finishes with a pointedly resigned-sounding, "She'll never change."

This man's intention is simply to tell his therapist about an unhappy and very difficult marriage situation of which he is, though trying to be hopeful, sometimes despairing. His repetition of the story and his emphasis, though, are unnecessary for that clear communicative purpose. By laying out the acts as he does, one gets the impression that, without quite realizing it, he is making a case, as if to someone who is not yet convinced. The case he is making, perhaps, is aimed to show that his hopes for a happy solution to his marital problem are unrealistic. Although he searches the therapist's eyes as he talks, he is not making this case only to convince the therapist, but rather to himself, hoping to find confirmation in the therapist's eyes.

At a clinical conference a female student therapist describes an unusual situation that has arisen in her treatment of a relatively new male patient. He is 25 years old, slightly built, somewhat effeminate, with an ingratiating, even obsequious, manner. In fact, he tells the therapist repeatedly that he is amazed at her ability to understand how he feels. He continues in this vein and goes further, still seemingly sincere, even suggesting, though he makes it clear it is "only a guess," that her parents were, perhaps, doctors and it may have been from them that she learned this wonderful capacity for empathy. The student therapist recognizes of course that the patient's reaction is overdone but, she wonders, what does it mean? Two opinions are offered at the conference: the first, that this is an expression of the patient's idealized image of the therapist: the second, that it is flattery, sincere, not cynical or calculating, but flattery.

The first opinion reflects an attention that is limited to what the patient says, that is, to the exaggerated picture that he draws, or constructs of the therapist. That exaggerated picture is seen simply as an expression of his exaggerated feelings and image of her. The content of his speech, in this view, is a reflection of the content of his mind. But the second opinion recognizes that the patient was doing something more than expressing the exaggerated picture that he had of the therapist and her capability. This opinion notes for example that the patient chose to tell the therapist about his idea of her capability, in fact to tell her repeatedly, even extending the exaggeration in the telling. He was not only saying something; he was doing something, even emphatically, by saying it. The image of the therapist is put to use for a further purpose, flattery, though not likely for her pleasure or self-satisfaction, but to satisfy or reinforce some image or role of his own.

> An elderly man, not well, sees his psychotherapist shortly after a visit to his physician. He enters the office with a grim expression, but the expression seems somehow prepared and the effect as he enters this way is of a person walking onto a stage. This does not seem like a performance only for the therapist, however, but an expression of his present idea of himself. The therapist remarks on his look as very sober. He responds with a reference to his appointment with the doctor and his explanation of his medical condition. He describes his doctor's attitude and the information he gave him with, again, a very grave, but noticeably exaggerated expression and, it seems, a pointed respect for certain of the doctor's observations. In this he seems to underline the threatening features of what was actually a mixed picture. When the therapist suggests as much, he responds by saying, with a kind of finality, "I have to face the facts."

What this man means by facing the facts is expecting and preparing himself for the worst. His statement, "I have to face facts," reflects his effort, sincere, but without full conviction, to believe what he thinks he should believe, that his fate is settled, and not to permit himself the indulgence and, for him, the anxiety of hope. The effort would be unnecessary if he actually believed that his fate was settled and there was no reason for hope.

Here is an example apart from the psychotherapy situation:

> A professor of sociology has just given a lecture before an academic group, and takes her seat next to a junior colleague. The younger woman praises the presentation in generally admiring terms, but in terms that are, also, somehow oddly specific in their evaluation. For example, she mentions noticing "a little problem at the beginning," but quickly adds, that the speaker had really "done very well" in recovering and presenting her thesis.

It is easy to understand why the presenter is annoyed at her younger colleague's comments. Apart from mention of the "little problem" at the beginning, the younger woman's comments, even when admiring and enthusiastic, constituted a review, an evaluation of the senior person's efforts, unrequested and in itself experienced as condescending. But the younger woman was sincere in her effort to admire, and if it did end in some condescension, that was almost certainly unconscious.

In each of these examples the individual, though sincere, does not fully believe what he or she is saying. The unnecessary repetition, the exaggeration, the emphatic earnestness all reflect the speaker's effort to achieve conviction. In these efforts one might say that they are each talking *at* the listener, but *to* themselves, trying to feel or believe what is not actually felt or completely believed, and in each case essentially unconscious of that effort. We may add here a note on the corresponding effect of self-deceptive speech on the listener that was mentioned in Chapter 2. In each of these cases the listener's experience is likely to be one of less than complete or satisfactory contact with the speaker. When the speaker is not completely behind what he is saying and doing, the sensitive listener often feels he is merely an observer of a performance.

I have focused in this chapter on the nature of speech as volitional, purposeful action and the kinds of subjective experience and conflict that may involve. I introduced this focus partly as a corrective of the psychoanalytic idea of the patient's speech as a product of tensions and impulses seeking their own expression. But that is only a branch of the larger problem in psychoanalysis and in some measure academic psychology as well. That is the absence of a satisfactory conception of volitional action in general, including its varieties of subjective experience. The problem arises in psychoanalysis out of its traditional conception of psychological dynamics, a conception of largely unconscious internal forces and agencies directing the individual according to the aims of these forces and agencies (Shapiro 1970). This is in contrast to the reality of the individual directing himself according to his aims, however halfhearted or distorted or infiltrated by contrary ones those aims may be. The conception had its justification in the nature of scientific discoveries of its time. Its persistence probably owes something to personal and political as well as scientific accidents of history. These surely include Wilhelm Reich's total alienation from psychoanalysis after *Character Analysis* and Hellmuth Kaiser's separation from the field during the prewar and war years. The problem has since been mitigated of course by various developments in and around psychoanalysis. These include the general humanizing tendency of psychoanalytic ego psychology and, more pointedly, the influence of European phenomenologists and existential psychoanalysts, introduced in America by Rollo May. To these one should add the influence of the more humanistic psychiatrists and psychologists less bound by psychoanalytic tradition including, notably, Karen Horney, Harry Stack Sullivan and, among the psychologists, Carl Rogers.

The most direct, explicit confrontation of the problem from within psychoanalysis has been that of Roy Schafer in his book *A New Language for Psychoanalysis* (1976). Schafer proposed to separate psychoanalysis from its traditional dynamics of internal forces and agencies and turn it into a psychology of personal action by revising its language, as his title indicates. Thus, he proposed replacing the nouns and adjectives that traditionally refer to the forces and agencies of psychoanalytic dynamics with verbs and adverbs, requiring, as they do, the assumption of active, purposeful direction by a person. The proposal is attractive for its promise of a solution to the theoretical and therapeutic problem by the rigorous implementation of a straightforward principle of language. But that is also, in my opinion, its downfall. The revision of language from traditional psychoanalytic descriptions of internal forces or mechanisms moving or restraining the person to actions *of* the person is often appropriate and corrective. It is easily applied, for example, to descriptions of relatively simple action for which the subject's responsibility is in one way or another avoided or disavowed. But it is less convincing and sometimes quite strained when applied to complex processes of defense or to emotional experiences. Thus, the replacement of "a projection" with "he projects" or "a regression" with "he regresses" does not seem particularly clarifying, and replacing "the idea of happiness by the idea of doing actions happily" (p. 277) treats as interchangeable two different phenomena. Schafer is insistent that the revisions and corrections that he proposes "are not descriptive, empirical propositions; they are definitions or rules that establish the logic of this psychological language" (p. 139). In this, he is adhering to a philosophical view that we are expected to accept. It seems to me, however, that replacing the conception of an internal mechanism as the responsible agent of a psychological effect with one of the individual's purposeful action is in fact a descriptive, empirical proposition. There is no doubt that the understanding of psychological dynamics in terms of individual action, including thought of course, is of critical theoretical and therapeutic importance, but that project requires not simply the application of language rules. It requires the analysis and concrete demonstration of how that action actually works. It is a matter for discovery, not stipulation.

References

Austin, J. L. (1962) *How to do things with words.* Cambridge: Harvard University Press.

Fenichel, O. (1941) *Problems of psychoanalytic technique.* New York: Psychoanalytic Quarterly Press.

Reich, W. (1949) *Character analysis.* New York: Orgone Institute Press.

Schafer, R. (1976) *A new language for psychoanalysis.* New Haven: Yale University Press.

Shapiro, D. (1970) Motivation and action in psychoanalytic psychiatry. *Psychiatry: Journal for the Study of Interpersonal Processes, 33*(3), 329–343.

Chapter 9

Voluntary surrender of responsibility

We have seen the retreat from or surrender of autonomy and personal responsibility as an anxiety-forestalling or dispelling, self-protective reaction both to external coercion and the internal conflict of psychopathology. These reactions are more or less reflexive self-deceptions. Their aims are unconscious and, in some measure, their subjective experience can only be inferred from their results. But now we turn to situations in which the surrender of autonomy and personal responsibility for what one says or does or believes is perfectly conscious, voluntary, and explicit. We have the opportunity therefore to see the process of such a surrender more clearly, to see that process, so to speak, in slow motion. The people we will consider are freely and knowingly eager to surrender personal direction and responsibility for what they say and do. One might even say of them that they are eager to achieve, at least conditionally, a mental state comparable, in their surrender of genuine conviction for formulaic "beliefs," to the mental state of people sincerely giving false confessions. Yet they do not face any coercive threat from which they must protect themselves.

There are innumerable situations in which this kind of voluntary surrender of autonomy and responsibility can be seen. I will take as my main examples here the devotees and recruits of two charismatic religious groups, the Hare Krishna group of the International Society for Krishna Consciousness (ISKCON) and the "Moonies" of Reverend Moon's Unification Church. In both cases the discussion will have in mind only full time members, not occasional participants living in their own homes. These groups, or cults, are useful for our discussion because they are quite open about their practices, especially their methods of developing and sustaining devotion. To these I have added a brief mention of another group that is at present of great international concern, the Islamic State (ISIS), to see if our understanding can be of use, also, in connection with its psychology.

Not surprisingly, these religious groups have often been charged with brainwashing their recruits and members. That charge has been made with great feeling, of course, by parents of young recruits and members, and they have had strong evidence in support of the charge. There are obvious likenesses in both the practices of these groups and their effects on recruits and members to those of the coercive situations mentioned in Chapter 2: the stereotyped behavior produced in the Chinese thought reform camps, and the Soviet show trials, the false confessions extracted under police interrogation, the doubtful recovered memories produced at therapists' insistence. There is, to begin with, the acceptance by the recruits and members of strange and radical ideas and practices—such as, for the followers of Reverend Moon, acceptance of him as the Messiah, arranged marriages, exclusion of previous relationships; for the Hare Krishna group, also, the exclusion of previous relationships together with renunciation of the material world, the acceptance of Krishna as God and the creator of the cosmos, the ritualistic chanting and ecstatic dancing, and, for both groups, acceptance of the authority and exaltation of leaders. But it is not only the content of the recruits' new ideas, which, after all, could probably be equaled in imaginativeness by familiar features of more conventional religions. More important is the abrupt and radical discontinuity from their earlier mental state in general. The attitudes of the recruits, even the ways they present themselves, seem to alter abruptly with their new association. The manner in which the new ideas and practices are expressed, conspicuous in its abrupt change, makes those ideas and practices suspect as the results of other than a genuine, considered change of mind.

Observers of both groups speak of the recruits' and members' fixed, formulaic responses to questions, their "dogmatic" or "parrot-like" explanation of their religion; their "glazed look" in conversation (Galanter 1999). In the case of the Moonies, it is their relentlessly happy and enthusiastic manner and display of affection ("love bombing") that "did not seem genuine" (Barker 1984). There is no suggestion in any of this of insincerity or deliberate deception of others, only of a lack of genuine conviction in the recruits and members themselves. It seems clear that they think they do believe in what they say and do, but what they say and do does not seem to others to carry conviction. What they say and do does not seem really theirs. Hence, the charge of brainwashing.

Nevertheless, these religious groups, or cults, have had effective defenders against the charge of brainwashing (Rochford 1985; Barker, 1984). In particular, that charge is refuted by a conspicuous and seemingly decisive difference from the brainwashing situation. It is that very difference that is the subject of this chapter: the abandonment of autonomous, critical thinking and direction in these groups is voluntary. It is not the reflexive, self-protective abandonment of autonomous thinking we see in the prisoner facing terrifying coercion or even the frightened subject of insistent bullying. For there is no coercive threat in the religious groups comparable to those situations. Those are all conditions of captivity that can easily be imagined to give rise to a level of anxiety that would impel a self-protective surrender of autonomy. It is true that in the religious groups there is what has been called a soft coercion. We shall consider that in a moment. And in the case of another religious group, the Scientologists, the coercive threat is not always that soft (Wright 2013). But the basic fact remains that those who join these groups, Scientology included, do so of their own volition. Their voluntary nature is underlined by the fact that most people who are invited to join refuse to do so. Those who do become recruits or members are free to leave at any time, and apparently most do. Indeed, both the Moonies and the Hare Krishna devotees seem to be much less in evidence than they were in the 1970s or 1980s.

The fact is, far from being coerced, the recruits' surrender of autonomy and suspension of critical judgment, as far as those can be achieved, is eager. The uncritical acceptance of the ideas and practices handed down for which there can be only a limited sense of personal responsibility, is far from passive. It is an active embrace. Recruits and devotees work hard, not critically, certainly, but hard, at this surrender of autonomy and at achieving belief. For example: a young woman devotee of Krishna Consciousness, quoted by Rochford, speaking of her efforts to separate from the material world, in particular from her boyfriend, says, "I was putting my whole heart and mind into Krishna. . . . I was chanting sincerely. . . . I want to actually realize that Krishna is God" (Rochford p. 119).

It is important to note that this Krishna devotee speaks of wanting "to actually realize" that Krishna is God. This is surely a different mental process from the cognitive one that normally leads to conviction or belief. Her attention is inward, on herself, on her own mind. Her effort is to create a sensation, a state of mind, in herself. She hopes to achieve that sensation and state of mind not, as with belief, by contemplating the external subject of interest, but by chanting.

However eager one may be, belief, conviction, cannot be summoned at will, not even by extreme effort. Nor can self-deception be. It is not possible to achieve that mental state in which critical judgment and purposeful thinking and experience of responsibility for what is said and done are surrendered simply by decision or deliberate, conscious wish, however urgent. Consciousness of the intention to do so would itself stand in the way. That mental state is involuntary; it requires certain conditions. We know of such a suspension or surrender of people's critical judgment, for example, when they are terrified, as in the Chinese thought reform camps, or even when they are intimidated. If this devotee's effort of surrender to Krishna relied only on her conscious wish, in the absence of the psychological conditions required for such a surrender, one would conclude that it was bound to fail. But in fact her effort included more than a simple conscious wish, however urgent. For she was "putting (her) whole heart and mind into Krishna" and "chanting sincerely." This formulaic recitation, repeated energetically and rhythmically over some period of time, constitutes not just the expression of a wish, but an incantation, a mantra. We do not know if it had the desired effect on this occasion, but we may presume that her previous experience of monotonous repetition of an incantation of this kind gave her some grounds for hope of achieving the desired mental state.[1]

I observed in the chapter on self-deception that brainwashing cannot be done directly. It is not a process in which one idea or point of view can be inserted in the subject's mind and another dissolved. Such a change requires a mediating step in which the normal interest in active, critical thought and judgment of reality is in some way disabled or caused to be suspended. The effects achieved in the charismatic religious groups bear out that conclusion. The conditions for achieving "belief" among these religious groups, including the two I have mentioned, vary in their particulars and in the intensity of their practices, but they share certain critical practices. These are aimed precisely, sometimes explicitly, at the abandonment or, in the term sometimes used in the groups themselves, the surrender of critical thought and judgment and autonomous self-direction in general.

The general aim of these special practices is, as I said, for the recruit or member not merely to be convinced of particular ideas, but to embrace a new state of mind. What is desired, or expected, is a passively accepting, unreflective, cognitive attitude, a relinquishing of personal judgment and control to another, a leader or teacher, or to the direction contained in the religious teaching. It is an attitude for which the term "surrender" is apt. Thus for the recruit in the Krishna Consciousness group the surrender of personal judgment includes not only an acceptance of the idea of Krishna as God and creator of the cosmos, but, also, the uncritical acceptance of the authority of the group's leaders and ideology. A total and exclusive emotional and cognitive immersion in and devotion to the principles and practices of Krishna Consciousness is expected. It is thought necessary "to destroy man's attachment to the world by shifting that affection . . . to the Lord . . . (to achieve devotion) that will occupy the whole self and absorb all of energies" (Gelberg 1989 p. 138).

How is this accomplished? The idea of "total immersion" speaks for itself. The general instruction or continuing requirement for the Krishna Consciousness devotees is to "constantly hear about, glorify, remember and worship the personality of Godhead" (p. 138). For example, the young Krishna devotee quoted above describes her experience with her guru: "I couldn't fight him . . . he would preach and preach every single day to me" (Rochford 1985). The effort at achieving belief through total immersion is supported by communal living. A sharp separation from the devotees' previous life, including relationships, is expected, and interest in the material world is discouraged and generally avoided. The devoted members of the Krishna Consciousness group are expected to chant 16 rounds of the mantra ("Hare Krishna, Hare Krishna, Hare Hare, Krishna Krishna . . .") a day, each round consisting of 108 repetitions, counted out on a string of beads.

The recitation of the mantra is noncommunicative speech. Even if it is said with reference to a deity, its aim is not to communicate, but to alter the speaker's state of consciousness, or, more specifically, to achieve or intensify the speaker's own religious experience. It is thought to clear the way for emptying the mind of critical thinking. Thus the mantra is in Sanscrit and its content is essentially meaningless to the devotee. Though the mantras in the religious groups do not typically have a comprehensible content ("Om, Om"), if they do, the devotee who chants may be instructed to avoid interest in that content and listen only to the ritualistically repeated sounds. In achieving its purpose of a deeper or higher spiritual state of mind, according to the group's conception, the chanting of the mantra sometimes leads to ecstatic singing and dancing. The experience seems not unlike the temporary state of excitement with singing, clapping and speaking in tongues in Pentecostal churches (Galanter 1999). Even if the goal of the mantra is mundane, such as prosperity or long life, as in some cases it may be, the means of reaching that goal is assumed to be the achievement of a special state of mind.

The Moonies, similarly, seek a total cognitive immersion in their religious dogma. Participants are expected to follow the Messiah, that is, the Reverend Moon, unquestioningly through disciplined prayer, fasting, and studying the "Divine Principle." Thus a devotee, described by Galanter (1999), is directed by his spiritual mentor to full-time prayer for 2 days during which he is to eat no solids. He says, "my body could sense that I was closer to liberation from my old concerns. The prayers soon developed a rhythm of their own . . . there was a pleasant loneliness I could almost feel" (p. 69). Here, too, there is an arrangement of communal living and, for the recruit, "near constant presence of enthusiastic Moonies" (Barker 1984 p. 174). Among the devotees, continuous love, happiness and enthusiasm are expected and, though of doubtful genuineness, these are shown unremittingly by devotees to recruits. Both the Hare Krishna and Moonie recruits are therefore surrounded by a relentless pressure of unanimous opinion and, equally relentless, the expectations and demands, constant preaching and urging, of leaders and teachers. Like the Krishna Consciousness group, separation from the world outside is urged for the Moonies, alternative viewpoints are excluded as "missing the truth," critical thinking in general is discouraged and the recruits' capability for independent judgment is disparaged. The Moonie recruit or devotee is exhorted not to let "Satan or evil spirits invade one's thoughts" (Barker 1984). Independent, critical thinking is therefore discouraged and weakened both by direct admonition and by separation from its normal external nutrients.

Despite these efforts to achieve and sustain the desired state of mind, it seems generally not to be lasting. As I mentioned, there have been large-scale defections from the charismatic religious groups. The impermanence of many members' devotion is not surprising. The necessity of continuous and strenuous effort by devotees to sustain their acceptance of the groups' programs itself implies an absence of stability. That impermanence may also be taken as a further example of the limits of self-deception in general.

The surrender of independent judgment, despite the efforts to achieve it, is probably never complete and, one suspects, never without a degree of self-consciousness.

Even so, it appears that membership in these groups does provide a significant relief of emotional distress, especially evident in the period immediately after joining, to many of its members. Former devotees speak of relief from the stresses of ordinary life. It is impossible to apportion the relative contributions to this relief of the various aspects of membership—the monotonous repetition of prayers or mantra, the isolation from previous relationships, the solidarity or closeness of affiliation with the group, emphasized by Galanter, the religious dogma—since it is apparent that the various factors influence each other and that all must contribute to the special mental state of surrender. As I have said, the voluntary nature of membership in these groups protect them from the charge of brainwashing in its usual meaning, but it seems clear that their effective cognitive state is similar to that of, say, false confession, which is, after all, also aimed at mitigating distress. It is interesting, in this connection, that a limited relief from stress is evidently achieved by the kinds of occasional personal meditation that are widely practiced nowadays, often with the help of a mantra.

Under certain conditions, we know, a liberation from personal responsibility can have an effect not just of relief of stress and anxiety, but of a desired excitement. Thus for the Hare Krishna devotees the gradual intensification of the ritualistic incantation ("Hare Krishna, Hare Krishna . . .") may culminate in a desired state of ecstatic singing and dancing. A similar state, probably also somewhat forced, of surrender of responsibility for action to another, supposed spiritual, agent is seen in the rite of speaking in tongues in Pentecostal churches. These kinds of surrender of responsibility, though dramatic, are conditional and temporary and in themselves of little social consequence. Not so, when such a state of mind extends to violence, as in some political movements. At present, for example, it seems to be the state of mind of the ISIS fighters.

As cruel and bloody as the destructiveness of the terrorist group ISIS is, it is surely a theatrical performance as well. But it is a performance of a special kind and it reflects a special mental state of its participants. Presumably this is not so of its leaders for whom the performance may be no more than cynically devised propaganda, a show aimed at terrorizing civilians and recruiting members. But for the regular ISIS fighters and recruits it cannot be mere propaganda; they are believers or, at least, they must think they are. There are two kinds of performances, the kind that are aimed purely at an external audience and the kind aimed, less consciously, at an effect on the performers themselves. The first is the kind one sees in a theater. The actors play their role, consciously trying to look like, perhaps even trying to feel like, they really believe in what they are saying and doing. But even while they make that effort they never completely lose sight of their main purpose, to produce an effect on the audience. The performance of the ISIS fighters is different. The main purpose, though less conscious, of this kind of performance is an effect on the performers themselves. The theatricality, the masks, the raised weapons, and the rest, are aimed not simply at terrifying others, but at feeling like terrorists, exciting themselves, creating and intensifying a sense of being heroic, religious fighters and martyrs. It is an effort to sustain and intensify a state of excitement, a self-deception.

A person whose attention and interest are in this way absorbed in an effort of that sort has for the time being lost a degree of the normal interest in objective reality. It is a state of mind in which the normal sense of oneself and of responsibility for what one says or does are suspended, a state that may be likened in these formal respects, and apart of course from its real circumstances and consequences, to that of the ecstatic singing and dancing of the charismatic religious cults or the speaking in tongues at Pentecostal churches. This is exemplified in the experience of a young Turkish jihadist who had been fighting with ISIS in the Middle East, reported by Ceylan Yeginsu in *The New York Times* (September 16, 2014): "When you fight over there it's like being in a trance. Everyone shouts, 'God is the greatest,' which gives you divine strength to kill the enemy without being fazed by blood and guts."

As this report on the jihadist makes clear, people in a psychological state of this sort are capable of action that would probably be unacceptable even to them in their normal mental state. It may provide little comfort at present but, judging by the evidence of those who have left cults or thought reform camps, the militant jihadists, also, are likely to come to their senses if, or when, their situation changes or they are removed from it.

The willing or eager, sometimes even excited surrender of responsibility by people in crowds has of course been well known and a subject of study for a long time, most notably by LeBon, at the end of the nineteenth century, and Freud, who built his theory of group dynamics on LeBon's descriptions (1896). The outstanding features of the psychology of crowds that they, and others since, describe are consistent with what we have seen: a diminished autonomy and responsibility for action. Thus, Freud (1958), quotes LeBon: "He [the person in the crowd] is no longer conscious of his acts," adding, "as in the case of the hypnotized subject . . . has ceased to be guided by his will" (p. 8). The condition is clearly understood by both Freud and LeBon to include the loss of a firm sense of external reality and of genuine conviction about it. As to the conditions that encourage that surrender in the case of the crowd, an explanation limited to interpersonal dynamics, specifically Freud's conception of a regressive relationship with the leader, must be considered incomplete. One thinks, for instance, of the mass rallies of the Nazis addressed by Hitler. The condition of a charismatic leader is met, certainly, but surrounded by hypnotizing spectacle: the lights, the sounds, the attitude of the already-prepared crowd itself, the forceful, repetitive speeches. All that is surely essential to the excitement and the suspension of critical thinking and genuine conviction.

It would be a mistake to think that the experience of diminished responsibility in groups or otherwise is simply one of freedom from constraints and inhibitions, as though permitting a true expression of the individual. That was not Freud's view; he saw the experience as the replacement of the constraint imposed by conscience by that imposed by the leader and the crowd. In fact, as we have seen in the instance of the cults, something close to the opposite of free expressiveness occurs. In those situations, the surrender of personal responsibility in favor of the authority of the cult and its leader means a loss of genuineness and the adoption of some artificial role in speech and action. Its result is a kind of cult-speech and cult-action. Both the relentless "love" of the followers of Reverend Moon and the ecstatic dancing and singing of the Hare Krishna devotees seem forced and self-conscious, lacking in genuine conviction. The same can be said of the supposedly abandoned behavior, speaking in tongues, of Pentecostal church services. The social critic Theodor Adorno (1991) makes the point in a striking way when, referring to the reaction of crowds to fascist leaders and propaganda, he says,

> The category of 'phoniness' applies to the leaders as well as to . . . the masses and their supposed frenzy and hysteria. Just as little as people believe in the depth of their hearts that the Jews are the devil, do they completely believe in their leader.
>
> (p. 131)

Adorno underscores this absence of genuine conviction by quoting Freud's remark, in regard to the comparable situation of the hypnosis, that the hypnotized subject knows, "that in spite of everything hypnosis is only a game." The frenzy of the crowds and the behavior of the hypnotic subject are, again, performances, but of the special kind I have described. They are performances in which the performer deceives himself that he believes in what he is doing.

Note

1 See the work on monotonous stimulation by I. E. Farber, H. F. Harlow and L. J. West (1957).

References

Adorno, T. (1991) *The culture industry: selected essays on mass culture.* In Freudian theory and the pattern of fascist propaganda. New York: Routledge.
Barker, E. (1984) *The making of a Moonie: choice or brainwashing?* Oxford: Blackwell.
Farber, I. E., Harlow, H. F., & West, L. J. (1957) Brainwashing, conditioning, and DDD (Debility, Dependency and Dread). *Sociometry, 20*(4), 271–285.
Freud, S. (1958) *Group psychology and the analysis of the ego.* New York: Hogarth Press.
Galanter, M. (1999) *Cults: faith, healing, and coercion.* Oxford: Oxford University Press.
Gelberg, S. (1989) Exploring an alternative reality: spiritual life. In G. D. Bromley & L. D. Shinn (Eds.), *Lewisburg ISKCON in Krishna consciousness in the West.* Lewisburg: Bucknell University Press.
Kaiser, H. (1955) The problem of responsibility in psychotherapy. *Psychiatry, 18*, 205–211.
LeBon, G. (1896) *The crowd: a study of the popular mind.* London: Ernest Benn.
Rochford, E. B. (1991) *Hare Krishna in America.* New Brunswick: Rutgers.
Wright, L. (1994) *Remembering Satan.* New York: Knopf.
Yeginsu, C. (September 16, 2014) *New York Times.*

Afterword: Action and responsibility

We are able, at this point, to see a consistency in all the various instances we have considered of the effects of the avoidance or surrender of responsibility for what one says and does and thinks. Let me list those effects: relief of emotional distress in the cult members; dispelling or forestalling of the anxiety of internal conflict in neurotic conditions, and mitigation of the anxiety or terror of external threat in the form of coercion or intimidation; excitement of a kind of liberation in certain group or crowd situations; impairment of purposeful, coherent thinking; and direction of attention in schizophrenia. The list comprises a great variety of individuals and situations and, therefore, also of effects. Yet all are effects of the person's estrangement from, and less than complete sense of ownership and direction of, what he, himself, does. Where the sense of ownership of what one says, does or thinks is surrendered or avoided by the individual, it is experienced by him to be elsewhere. For the person under the sway of what he "should" think or do, for example, responsibility is shared with seemingly authoritative internal, quasi-moral rules. For others, responsibility is assigned to some authoritative external figure or movement, or to the urgency of one's immediate emotional reaction or "impulse," or, in schizophrenia, to some compelling associative thought or idea. In these ways, the person, the author of the thought or action, hides, and is hidden from himself. We may note that in its most subtle form, this phenomenon is what Hellmuth Kaiser (1955) observed, and we described at the beginning of this book, as a certain artificiality in his patients. They seemed quite sincere, but they did not know what they really believed or felt or wanted to do. We remember, though, that all these kinds of self-estrangement are incomplete. What is hidden is not gone, but only, at least for the time being, out of reach.

Index

act of decision 68
action:
   autonomy and 1
   impulses and 52
   spontaneous 52–53
   versus temptation 3
   volitional 66, 91, 109
   see also speech, purposeful
addiction 62
Adorno, Theodor 127–128
Angyal, A. 99
Arieti, Silvano 98–100
artificiality 5–6, 30, 33, 129
attention, difficulties with 91–92
Austin, J. L. 109, 111
autonomy:
   action and 1
   surrender of 37
   see also voluntary surrender of responsibility

Beerbohm, Max 78
Bleuler, E. 92
brainwashing 35–36, 120–121, 122

catatonic schizophrenia 98–99
change, lack of 106–107
Chapman, J. 90, 91, 92, 93
Character Analysis (Reich) 106, 109, 115
Chinese thought reform 36–37, 38, 102, 120, 122

choice:
   anxiety of 80–81
   conscious 3, 52
   personal 16–17
   reality of 68
   will and 69–73
civil rights activists 54
coercion 8, 35–36, 37, 38, 120–121
conceptual goals of the ego 108
Confession, The (London) 38
conscientiousness:
   of conviction 9
   of rules 8–9
   two kinds of 8, 41–49
   see also obsessive indecision
conscious choice 3, 52
consciousness raising 27–28
conviction, conscientiousness of 42, 43, 44–45
crowds, psychology of 126–128
Cutting, J., 93 100

decision, act of 68
defenses/defense mechanisms 55, 77–78, 80
deliberateness:
   avoidance of 83
   consciousness of choice and 52
   development of 2
   increased consciousness of 24
determinism 65–66, 69, 72–74
Diagnostic Statistical Manual of Mental Disorders (DSM-5) 51

disavowal of responsibility 7, 9–10
distractibility 91–92, 93
dogmatic people 33, 43
double bookkeeping 100
drives. *see* needs, impulses, drives, and wishes
dual thinking process 100
Dunne, F. 93, 100
Dynamics of Character (Shapiro) 11

early cognitive development theory 55
ego, conceptual goals of 108
empathic understanding 17, 18–19, 48–49
existential psychoanalysts 116

failures of impulse control 9–10
false confessions 8, 11, 35–38, 119, 120, 125
Farber, Leslie 65, 66
Fenichel, Otto 108, 110, 111
Flechsig, Dr. 96, 97
free will 10, 65–75
Freud, Sigmund 55, 77, 94, 96, 105, 126–128
Frith, C. D. 92

Galanter, M. 124, 125
Goldstein, Kurt 65
group dynamics 126–128

Hare Krishna group 119–120, 121–123, 124, 125, 127
Holzman, Philip 89
Horney, Karen 116
humanistic psychiatrists and psychologists 116
hypnosis 127–128
hysterical character 83–86

illocutionary force 111–112
immersion, religious groups/cults and 122–124

impetuous people 56, 79
impulse control, failures of 9–10
impulse-control disorders 51
impulses. *see* needs, impulses, drives, and wishes
impulsive people 52–53, 86
indecision 4–5, 8, 83, 98
infants 1–2
intellectual insight 106
International Society for Krishna Consciousness (ISKON) 13, 119–120, 121–123, 124, 125, 127
Islamic State (ISIS), 119–120, 125–126

Johnson, David Read 98

Kaiser, Hellmuth 5–6, 15–16, 30, 37, 86, 115, 129
Knight, Robert P. 72

Lakoff, Robin T. 83
LeBon, G. 126–127
Lifton, R. J. 36–37
London, Artur 38

mantras 34–35, 122, 123–124, 125
Matussek 93
May, Rollo 65, 66, 116
McGhie, A. 90, 91, 92, 93
Memoirs of My Nervous Illness (Schreber) 96
Moon, Sun Myung 13, 119–120, 124, 127
Moonies 119, 120, 121, 124, 127
moral accountability/moral sense of responsibility 7–8, 9, 16, 41, 48–49, 67–68
moral judgment development of, 42–43
moral reproach 17

needs, impulses, drives, and wishes 3–4, 12, 51–52, 56

neurotic styles 77–87
Neurotic Styles (Shapiro) 11
New Language for Psychoanalysis, A (Schafer) 116
nonviolence, self-control and 54

obsessive indecision 4–5, 8, 83, 98
obsessive-compulsive style 79, 80–81

paranoid people 81–83, 94–97, 100–101
passively reactive styles 79–80, 91
Pentecostal churches 125, 126, 127
personal authority, disavowal of 83–84
phenomenologists 116
Piaget, Jean 42
psychoanalytic method 105–106, 115–116
psychological determinism 65–66, 72–74
psychological meaning of responsibility 7–8, 16
psychopaths 55–56
psychosis 33
psychotherapy, fundamental assumptions of 68–69

radical Islamic movement 13, 119–120, 125–126
reality of choice 68
Reich, Wilhelm 5, 12, 30, 106–108, 109, 115
religious groups/cults 119–125, 127
responsibility:
    disavowal of 7, 9–10
    exaggerated sense of 15
    moral sense of 7–8, 9, 16, 41, 48–49, 67–68
    two kinds of 7–8, 15–25
    voluntary surrender of 13, 119–128
restraint 53–56
retreat 6–7, 11
rigid styles 79–83, 90–91

Rochford, E. B. 121
Rogers, Carl 116
rules, conscientiousness of 42, 43–44

Sass, Louis 93, 100
Schafer, Roy 116
schizophrenia 11–12, 89–102
Schreber, Daniel Paul 94, 96–98
Schrodinger, Erwin 73
Scientologists 121
scrupulosity 99, 101
Sechehaye, M. 93–94, 100, 101
self-control 9–10, 51–63
self-deception:
    defenses and 78, 84
    disavowal of responsibility and 9–10, 51
    limits of 124–125
    overview of 8
    psychology of 27–38
    shame and 47–48
    see also schizophrenia
self-estrangement 16
self-protective actions 11, 12, 30–31, 90–91, 97
    see also defenses/defense mechanisms
self-reproach 17–18, 20–25, 44
shame 7–8, 9, 16, 41, 42, 44, 45–49
Shaw, George Bernard 78
sociopaths 53, 55–56
soft coercion 121
Soviet-style show-trials 38, 120
speaking in tongues 125, 126, 127
speech:
    purposeful 12, 105–117
    ritualistic 37
    self-deceptive 30–35
subjective experience:
    lack of study of 2–3
    speech and manner and 2
suggestive people 33
Sullivan, Harry Stack 116

Tahka, V. 99
talk therapy 105–111
temptation:
   versus action 3
   willpower and 66–67
threats, signaling of 28–29

Unification Church 13, 119–120, 121, 124, 127

values self-control and, 54
volition 16–17
volitional action 66, 91, 109
volitional level 59
voluntary surrender of responsibility 13, 119–128

Werner, Heinz 32
Wheelis, Allen 65, 66
will 10, 65–75
willpower 10, 53, 65–75
wishes. *see* needs, impulses, drives, and wishes

Yeginsu, Ceylan 126